AM I READY NOW?

AM I READY NOW?

7 Principles Identifying You're Ready to Walk Into the Fulfillment of Your Life

Dr. Donnell D. Cunningham

ELM HILL

A Division of
HarperCollins Christian Publishing

www.elmhillbooks.com

© 2019 Dr. Donnell D. Cunningham

Am I Ready Now?
7 Principles Identifying You're Ready to Walk Into the Fulfillment of Your Life

All rights reserved. No portion of this book may be reproduced, stored in a retrieval system, or transmitted in any form or by any means—electronic, mechanical, photocopy, recording, scanning, or other—except for brief quotations in critical reviews or articles, without the prior written permission of the publisher.

Published in Nashville, Tennessee, by Elm Hill, an imprint of Thomas Nelson. Elm Hill and Thomas Nelson are registered trademarks of HarperCollins Christian Publishing, Inc.

Elm Hill titles may be purchased in bulk for educational, business, fund-raising, or sales promotional use. For information, please e-mail SpecialMarkets@ThomasNelson.com.

All Scripture quotations, unless otherwise indicated, are taken from the King James Version. Public domain.

Library of Congress Cataloging-in-Publication Data

Library of Congress Control Number: 2019909415

ISBN 978-1-400326594 (Paperback)
ISBN 978-1-400326600 (eBook)

DEDICATION

I dedicate this book to my spiritual father, the Right Reverend, His Grace the late Bishop Robert L. Bussey. Dad, thank you for seeing beyond Donnell and recognizing who God had called me to be, for such as time as this.

Acknowledgments

To God be the glory! I give him all glory, praise, and thanks for His spiritual guidance and direction through this process. Without His word and His spirit this project would have never been birthed. I pray that this book and my testimony alone inspire, motivate, and persuade the masses to submit to His holy will. I thank you, God, for your divine inspiration in allowing me to put your words on paper, which will bring many back to you, willing to do all it takes to serve you wholeheartedly, crying out, "Lord, I'm ready now!"

To my grandmother, I love you, and I want to honestly thank you for pointing me in the right direction to follow Christ through the good and the bad. To Shantrelle and Anthony, know Dad loves you and is thankful to be blessed with such great children. I want you to remember that in spite of everything all things are possible through Christ our Lord. Never be ashamed of your testimony! To my sister and confidant Shanta, I love you dearly and want to personally thank you for your prayers, love, dedication, endless support, and loyalty. You prove the word that states we are more than conquerors! To my nieces Tyresa and Shainia, as well as my nephew Shyheim, Uncle loves you dearly and thanks you for your love and support. Remember you have the victory in Jesus' name to accomplish all your hopes and dreams.

To my number one associate Devonna Graham and the New Genesis Total Praise Center congregation, I love you. Thank you for supporting me and encouraging me to use my testimony as words to motivate and lead others to Christ. I urge each and every one of you to continue staying faithful in your walk daily, and do not despise small beginnings, for in time you, too, shall reap if you faint not.

And to you who felt led to purchase this book, I want to thank you as well. You have no idea of the journey this book will take you through to help shape and mold you into who God has called you to be. Don't worry about your past but use it as a motivating factor to push you into your destiny, for in time you shall be revealed as a new creature in Christ.

Introduction

Let me ask you, "Are you ready?" You might be asking yourself, "Ready for what?" Or maybe the better question is, "Are you tired of running?" You see, my friend, readiness in all actuality is a state of preparedness. So I ask you, "Are you prepared to make the move that will allow you to fulfill your purpose?" So often we get spooked into believing we have to have this and we have to have that to do what God wants us to do. It has been drilled into our heads that in order to serve God this is needed or that should be obtained, so instead we delay our path to our purpose. And yet all God needs is a simple yes. So I ask you, beloved, look deep within your heart, soul, and mind, and ask yourself this one personal question: "Am I ready now?" Be truthful, because only you know the answer to this question. Sincere honesty is needed. Once you give him an honest, heartfelt yes, then the rest will come. The willingness of your mind to give God a complete yes opens the door to letting God know you are ready, ready to do his will and fulfill your purpose. But many of us, like myself, find ourselves running in fear of what this "yes" really means and how it will affect our lives and what we, not God, want to do.

So we get caught up in pleasing people, doing ungodly things, hanging around in unhealthy and unproductive environments, where we let the world drag us further and further away from who we, as children of the most high king, have been called to be, leading us to a place where we have lost our identity, sense of being, and focus. Which then causes us to start slipping down into a blurry, murky path of self-destruction and disobedience, jeopardizing our lives, minds, and our kingdom placement. I myself can identify with this deadly and dreaded path and will tell you once you allow the enemy to push you down into this pit of misery, it is difficult to escape. It was not until I realized like the prodigal son that my Heavenly Father had so much to offer me than the world and in him I could have joy, safety, productivity, and hunger no more, I found myself running back to him with open arms, saying, "I yield and surrender."

And you, too, can find safety and deliverance from that which has had you bound using these seven principles. They will help lead and guide your walk into the fulfillment of your life as you answer the nagging question, "Am I ready now?"

Contents

1	**The Call**	1
	Principle #1: You Can Run but You Can't Hide!	10
2	**Defeating Distractions**	17
	Principle #2: You've Got to Come to Yourself!	24
3	**Identifying Counterfeit and Authentic**	29
	Principle #3: Honesty Is the Best Policy!	34
4	**Message from the Mess**	41
	Principle #4: Pitfalls Lead You to the Call!	47
5	**The Acceptance of God's Will**	51
	Principle #5: God Has No Respect of Person!	
	(Status, Title Don't Matter!)	55
6	**There's Purpose in the Process**	61
	Principle #6: Where You Are Is Not a Coincidence!	67
7	**The Revealing**	77
	Principle #7: You Shall Come Forth!	86
	Conclusion: The Decision	91

CHAPTER 1

THE CALL

Life is simply an adventure waiting to happen. But along with the adventure comes mazes that try to deter, stop, or even alter the path that God personally destined for you. And you may find yourself trapped, lost, or even confused as you desperately seek direction, clarity, or even guidance on which path you should take, hoping it brings you to an end. But how many know that in the maze of life it takes time, focus, and a strong sense of direction to really find your way? And as I reflect on my own life, I don't know about you who may be reading this book, but honestly my life has been all but ordinary. Speaking of myself, my life has been a maze with twists, turns, dead ends, restarts, unexpected surprises, and a path that at times may have looked dark, bleak, gloomy, and confusing. What about you? I'm amazed and awed today at my progress and how far I've come. I sit back and reflect, still questioning just exactly how I made it through the treacherous and adventurous maze of what we call life, but thanks be to God for his grace and his mercy. I honestly do not know where I would be if it had not been for God's loving-kindness and his never-ending interest in a man such as myself. As matter of fact we should all be so elated that regardless of how many times we've gotten lost or distracted in the maze of life, we can overcome to get to the place where God wants us to be if we decide to yield to his will and his way. See, God is the only one I know who can take something that is trashy, invaluable, and undesirable and remake it into something so beautiful and authentic one can no longer recognize what it originally may have been. He is a miracle-working God, and through his divine will we are made whole. For some of us when we look back over our lives and reminisce about out past, we realize we've come too far to turn back now.

See, what you may not know is when you have a call on your life the enemy will try to deter you from your call and cause an interference. Similar to cell phone towers and how phone calls are generated through them when an interference comes, it can cause issues with your service such as:

- Dropped calls
- Unclear calls
- Unavailable service

But for me, who would have thought Satan would try to run an interference when I was at the tender age of two? The only reason I can think of is because he literally took a peak at my future and became threatened. But let me tell you, Satan, you slew-footed fool, nothing you tried worked because here I am today still standing! Isn't it funny how the devil believes he has the final say over what shall come forth in our lives? But let me tell you beloved, he doesn't. Satan, your service has been dropped!

He tried to kill me off, but it didn't work. The enemy must have seen the purpose and call God had set upon my life and was determined to stop my existence as we knew it, to prevent my destiny. I was just three months short of my third birthday when I was rushed to the hospital on September 30, 1977. Neither my grandmother nor my parents could figure out what was wrong with me and were worried sick. I laid on my mother's lap partially responsive, staring blankly back at her as they sped to the hospital. It had happened so suddenly and no one could figure out what was wrong with me. I was slowly slipping from this world and into the arms of Christ without even having the chance to experience the fullness of life and all it had to offer me. Upon reaching the hospital, doctors snatched me from my mother's arms without giving her, my father, or grandmother the opportunity to kiss me and tell me it would be better soon. The test results were inconclusive, and doctors were baffled as they stared at a two-year-old baby unable to move, talk, or even blink.

You see, Satan thought he had the victory. But he did not have the final say, God did. The doctors agreed it would be best to transfer me to Mt. Washington's Pediatric Hospital hoping the array of specialty pediatric doctors could save my life and bring me back to my family. Doctors and nurses entered my room around the clock, endlessly trying to save me, and it was revealed through in-depth neurological image testing that I had suffered a traumatic brain injury, which was the cause of my vegetative state, confusion, low-cognitive activity, leaking of blood from my nose, slow speech, and asthmatic attacks. Much prayer and much faith were the keys that kept my family strong and sane as they watched me constantly, day and night, lying there in the hospital bed with a feeding tube down my throat as fluids constantly kept me hydrated. The doctors had given me a low survival rate, making it clear I would remain in a vegetative state for the rest my life since test results revealed a fifty-five percentage of brain damage. But what they did not know was God was preparing to make me whole again. See, the devil saw the destiny God had for my life and he thought he would be able to take me out. But on December 1, 1977, he got the worst surprise of his life. Through the prayers of my family and community members I rose up stronger than ever, was fully functioning, and in my right mind. It took time, patience, and God's divine healing power; I recovered and had managed to gain an additional ten pounds. The day I left the hospital was the day Satan realized he could not interfere with God's divine plan for the call he had placed upon a life such as mine.

Truth be told we all have a call and Satan tries to deter us, because he has peeked into our lives and seen the plans God has for us. And Satan being who he is, he has probably tried to stop us through sickness, poverty, disappointment, divorce, loss of job, death of a loved one, and more, bringing you to a place where we find ourselves probably believing life is not what we imagined, pictured, or so-called "planned" for.

As a matter of fact you might be questioning just how in the world your life turned out the way it did, and why is it this way. Or maybe you are wishing for things to change. Yet I ask you, have you made any effort for a change to take place?

You see, saints, in all reality where we are standing today is the place we allowed ourselves to either venture in, wander into, or be led to. And you'd be surprised how many times we give the excuse "Such and such made me do it," "I'm doing the best I can," or "I'm trying." One of the best excuses I hear over and over as a pastor is, "God knows my heart." You can repeatedly play the blame game by claiming anything and everything delayed you from any kind of progress or accomplishment, but I ask you, as the apostle Paul asked in Galatians 5:7, "Who did hinder you?" This simple question suggests to all of us it is time to take a good look in the mirror and do a self-reflection. This is your reality check, because that person you see in the mirror looking back at you is who you should blame. Who else do you see?

And like Paul I ask you again, who hindered you? You know the answer. It's time to be truthful and just admit it.

When I look in the mirror, besides the fine, gorgeous creation of God I see, no matter all my frustrations, temptations, decisions, and such, I see the person I should be blaming: Donnell. See, it was me who made the bold decision to allow my life to spiral out of control, and it could have been my decision to allow my life to be as God had ordained and planned it to be. But I let temptation, curiosity, and just plain disobedience take me away from my rightful position and place in God. And it's all because I allowed the enemy to play me out of my position and rightful place in God. And you know how he did it: he used my emotions. Emotions are key to expressing how we as humans experience and feel, but they are also a curse when used as a weapon to express or demonstrate frustrations, irritations, irrational and illogical ideas.

See, where we all mess up is we let our human emotions take reign over our thoughts, thus the decision-making process becomes clouded and based upon how "we feel" rather than what we know. And so begins the dreaded life of confusion, pain, and anger that reign over our minds, spirits, and souls, eventually leading us down a path to a place of irrational thinking, indecisive thoughts, and chaotic reactions that take us farther away from who we really are in Christ. Which takes us down a path of unclear thinking and we become mentally unstable, finding ourselves in a place of double-mindedness. "A double minded man is unstable in all his ways" (James 1:8). This is a place where no one needs to be found in, because instability is a breeding ground for the works of the devil. Satan is ever searching for those he can redirect and deter from the will of God. He plots and seeks out those who are weak-minded, so he can destroy them. Whenever one is in a foolish, double-minded state we mistakenly allow our feelings and emotions to overtake our thoughts, becoming actions that we regrettably oblige. Which then brings us to a backward state of mind, where we find ourselves lost and confused, literally running backward, unable to function fully as a stable-minded human, pushing us away from the call of Christ and into a place of uncertainty. And speaking for myself it is a dangerous thing to run from Christ and his calling, because it leaves you in a place you really don't want to be in.

So, you may be asking about this "call" I keep alluding to and why it is so important for my life. You might be questioning if you have a call, or how you would know that you might have been called. Someone else might be wondering if this is a "call" only for the ones designated by God to preach his gospel. But let me be clear and help you by first informing you that as Christians we are called by God, our heavenly father, to obey his will and follow him. The word clearly states, "And he said to them all, If any man will come after me, let him deny himself, and take up his cross daily, and follow me" (Luke 9:23). He is beckoning each and every one of us to make the ultimate sacrifice by denying ourselves our own selfish human desires and taking that step of faith to follow him. It is that moment when God beckons us to serve him wholeheartedly. That momentous and glorious instance when he pushes on your heart to give him all of you or none of you, and you must decide whether you are ready to boldly exclaim yes or cowardly whisper no. Now I should let you know God calls no two people the same way, nor uses the same spiritual moment, but his calling to you comes at an instance, when he decides it is time to bring you into the safety and comfort of his will. He sends out the tender call like a shepherd looking after his sheep. See, he knows each one of us just like a shepherd knows each and every sheep in his flock, but he gives us the freewill to run to him or run from him. However, I should warn you, as in my case, no matter how far you run or think you can run, you can't outrun God.

Do you really think you can outrun God? I know someone is probably saying you can ignore him and do your own thing, but let me tell you, God cannot be silenced or ignored. He is like the prodigal son's father, waiting, seeking, and patiently anticipating your return to him, and he is calling your name. If you refuse, as in my case, to heed to his beckoning call he will lose patience, so be prepared for what may come your way. You could possibly lose more than just your material possessions; there is high chance your life is at stake. It is a dangerous thing to tell God no, especially when he holds the power of eternity in his hands. Do you not know that you could possibly be diminishing a meaningful and plentiful life that has been originally intended for you because you refuse to submit to his calling? God will only wait so long before he takes action to have his will done.

For every action there is a reaction. Have you ever been to the doctor for a physical examination? When they walk into the examination room they proceed to listen to your heartbeat, check your blood pressure, and get an accurate body temperature. Afterward the doctor will look into your ears and pull out the mechanism that tests your body reflexes. They will hit your knee and wait for your leg to perform a spontaneous kick before moving to the opposite leg. That is how God works; he waits before he reacts and gives time before he responds to the situation at hand.

Many in the Bible have suffered repercussions from not obeying God's request. One of the best examples is the pharaoh. He was a man of power, status, and wealth; God did not fear him. No matter your standpoint in life, whether it is one of wealth, prestige, or notoriety, when God has a call for you, you must answer. God simply took charge of the situation when the pharaoh refused to give in to God's plea and took what he wanted—the pharaoh's son's life, to get his point across. Do you still think you can play hide and seek with God? He wins every time. God has the power to orchestrate how things go in order to get you to the place where you yield your own will for his. And I am warning you, speaking from personal experience, what God wants he will get one way or another. This is why Jesus Christ said, "Nevertheless not my will, but thine, be done" (Luke 22:42) as he sojourned in the garden of Gethsemane, preparing to undertake one of the greatest but frustrating tasks of his life. With the weight of the world upon his shoulders he decided to forsake his own will to accomplish the hefty call upon his life.

And I can let you know, beloved, I thought I could outrun my call, ignore my call, remake myself into someone else to avoid the call. But no matter where I went or what I attempted to do God always found me. And I want to let you know he will find you, too, and when he does be prepared.

So I ask you, are you ready for the call? Me, I was never ready for the call and I have never been ashamed to openly admit that to anyone. For me it is a part of my testimony that I can boldly share with everyone. It took a lot of prodding from God and much prayer for me to accept his calling on my life. For those who know my testimony or have heard it, this is the side you do not know. Yes, I was called at an early age to proclaim the gospel of Christ and minister his word, but as I look back and reflect I realize now I was only imitating what I saw. You see, I grew up in the Church, was raised by a God-fearing grandmother, knew the word of God, was saved, sanctified, and filled with the Holy Ghost, yet secretly I refused to accept his calling on my life. I was afraid to completely commit and surrender to God. I was unsure of who I was in Christ fully, but the more he kept calling me the faster I ran. I was a mere adolescent entering my teen years, still running and denying who I was in Christ, refusing to accept his plan for my life. But as I ran a change came about in me, and I found myself acting out, entering a state of rebellion where I became disobedient, was fighting, and misbehaved on numerous occasions. At that time I was more fearful of what God wanted from me, and regardless of the prophecies that came I refused to yield and it showed through my rebellious state and actions. Yes, pride took part in that, but fear was the main culprit and its sidekick was ignorance.

You know, saints, it is so funny how we let the devil use fear and our lack of knowledge to lead us from the place God has for us and down a path that causes us to lose so much, knowing we cannot afford to lose anything, especially since the scripture clearly states, "My people are destroyed for lack of knowledge: because thou hast rejected knowledge" (Hosea 4:6). But there comes a time when we need to realize God is large and he is in charge. Despite how we may feel, how we see things, what we want, or how we desire things to go, when God has had enough he has had enough. And, saints, little did I know running was about to take my life into another dimension, where God was determined not only to prove who was in charge but that his preordained divine will was the only choice for survival.

What do you do when God wants you to turn left and you want to turn right? Do you immediately give in, or do you stubbornly refuse? Is it possible to even attempt to bargain with God? How can you surrender to the call of Christ when you think you're not ready? God, is this really what you want from me?

Principle #1
You Can Run but You Can't Hide!

When you make the decision to run from the call of God and not to his call, as in my case, it leads you to a place of confusion, rebellion, and loss of identity. You will find yourself unsatisfied and displeased with everything that occurs in your life, to the point you become frustrated. It's that moment when frustration sets in that you find yourself lost, and it is at that instant when you are most vulnerable that God steps in and takes charge. But his taking charge is not one of salvation but more of a thrust delivering you further into a dreary, lost, and dark place, where you have the option to either finally come to yourself and submit or to boldly proclaim no and continue running in a reprobate state of mind. Saints, when you refuse to heed the call of Christ on your life and proceed to run, it puts a target on your back like a huntsman searching for their game. And there is no more dangerous place to be in but that of someone who has been called by God and still running from his will.

But how many know you cannot run from God? See, he will get your attention any way possible to stop you, because when God has an assignment for your life be prepared to accept it willingly, or unwillingly. You will do his will, one way or another. It is his desire that you answer his call, and from personal experience God knows how to demonstrate just who is in charge. But in the end, when all is said and done and you're debating in your mind what your final decision will be, he leaves that to us. See, he's omnipotent for a reason, because he knows us, and he knows just exactly what move we are planning on making before we even know. But he requires of us that we "...seek him with all thy heart and with all thy soul" (Deuteronomy 4:29). And when we actually seek him with our whole heart and soul he is able to lead and direct us, but remember, when one tells God "no" he always has a way of making you in his perfect timing tell him yes. Just ask Brother Jonah. See, he thought he could escape and answer "no," but we all know what happened to him. He is a prime example of someone called by God to do his will. But he, like myself, decided to run until God got his full attention and cooperation.

Jonah, a minor Prophet, was minding his own business when he got his assignment and call from God to travel to the land of Tarshish and cry out against their sinning. You know many of us, if not only me, have found ourselves in a familiar place. We are living our lives without a care until we get that call from God to serve him and do his will. That is when we begin to question ourselves and ponder if we should obey the voice of God or keep going as if we never heard it. Might I suggest, saints, that when God calls you better answer and do it immediately! But we, like Jonah, disagree with God's agenda and call for our lives. How can we be so foolish as to disagree with the will of God? Are you God? Can you do what he does? I suggest do not be like Jonah to the point you consider telling God, "No!"

So Brother Jonah decided to purchase a ticket upon a cruise ship headed in the opposite direction. Isn't that something you've considered? Running to avoid any responsibility expected of you. I think it is time for you to realize the excuses and the avoidance of accepting any kind of responsibility has become a hindrance for you instead of a help. Running away profits you nothing when God has a task for your life. I thought I could run and hide from the call he set upon my life, but like Jonah's cruise trip it was a bad idea. God got angry, a storm broke out, and everyone feared for their lives while brother Jonah was fast asleep. Did you know running from your calling does not affect just you but also those around you? Jonah failed to realize that there were others around him who would be affected if he did not heed the call of Christ on his life. If he had neglected those around him there was a possibility Jonah would have been responsible for the consequences; they suffered under his carelessness. And, beloved, do you want to be that selfish person who decides running is more important that you'd be willing to risk the lives and souls of those around you because of your negligence and immaturity?

He awakened, realized God sent the storm, and suggested they throw him overboard, which they did immediately. I warn you now, you can be lazy, reluctant, even asleep on God and your calling, but dire circumstances will arise. Lack of commitment and enthusiasm for your assignment brings storms that result in you having to make an ultimate sacrifice: your life. We forget that with every bad decision comes a consequence, and they can get quite costly. If you value your life I suggest you take the call God has set upon you seriously and "Know ye not that they which run in a race run all, but one receiveth the prize? So run, that ye may obtain" (1 Corinthians 9:24). Keep focused and run this race with much faith and much motivation. Don't be so idle that you sleep on God's will for your life and lose your life in the balance. He's thrown into the sea, swallowed by a large fish, and Jonah remained there for three days and nights until he decided to seek God and apologize. Because of God's mercy and grace, he gave one last chance before sending destruction or punishment to those who decided they wanted to run from their calling. It is an opportunity that should be taken seriously and graciously, as a chance to get oneself together by doing as Jonah did. You see, grace never lasts always and God can snatch it away, allowing you to experience firsthand life without his kindness and favor.

He sat in that fish's belly and he came to himself, realizing that serving God and obeying his will for his life was better than death, entrapment, and bondage. He was filled with a spirit of repentance that brought about humility and obedience, causing him to seek God and pray. Folks, God does not always give second chances, so when he does I suggest we get right with God by making things correct immediately. It took Jonah almost losing his life to realize God was not playing with him, and it was a must he surrender to the call of Christ Jesus on his life. I urge you and plead with you to take the time today to give God a yes, for as we say, tomorrow is never promised. He was then regurgitated back onto the shore and went to fulfill the call of Christ upon his life without a reasonable doubt from that day forward. Do you really want to go the long way with all bumps, hiccups, potholes, and traffic, or would you prefer to take the direct route? I learned that God does give man the option to choose, but when it comes to doing his will and following his way, there is but one option: God's.

Can you imagine if Jonah had simply told God yes? As a matter of fact, can you imagine if you submit and give God a yes? There is power in your words and you need to take hold of that power to take up your cross and follow Christ. Do not be ashamed of your fear, worry, or doubt; instead it is time for you to stand strong and give the devil a run for his money. Maybe it's your time and your season to get yourself together and fully commit to God, but you keep thinking, "I just need more time, I'm not ready yet." I thought the same thing until he turned everything around me into a dangerous, treacherous storm that could not be easily calmed or ceased. It was then that I, too, like Jonah, realized it was not worth the energy, time, or costliness to keep letting myself run ragged in a storm I possibly could not survive. And in this instance I had only one choice, and that was to boldly exclaim, "Lord, save me!" You see, what we all fail to realize, my sisters and my brothers, is that God has a divine will and purpose for all of our lives, but he gives us the choice to decide if we want to accept his call to service or deny it. But I must let you know, from my personal experience, that God does not take "no" lightly or as your final answer.

But God being who he is, our father, he sits back and observes as we either take the road that leads to blessings and breakthroughs or the road that leads to demise and destruction. And we in our foolish reprobate states of mind allow these choices to cause us loss of focus, reality, and identity, pulling us into a downward swirl of darkness, misconception, uncertainty, and unfamiliarity.

The word states, "…for wide is the gate, and broad is the way, that leadeth to destruction, and many there be which go in thereat" (Matthew 7:13). Yes, God does send warning before destruction, but in this state of spirituality a war has already commenced. The war between God's desire for your total submission to do his will and Satan's desire for you to do his. So the quandary is not just whose will you decide to do but your willingness to answer the call in doing so.

As humans one of the greatest enemies we must to learn to face is fear. It is an enemy that has been in existence since the beginning of time and still taunts and wreaks havoc in our minds, which in turn overtakes our thinking process. But now is the time for us to come out from the entrapment of fear and stand still, knowing that fear can no longer hold us bound from fulfilling the destiny God has specifically created and shaped for us. It is time to come to ourselves, shake ourselves free from the bounds of fear, worry, anxiety, and stand strong in knowing who we are and who God has called us to be.

If you make the first step by admitting "you are ready" for a change in your life to God, I can guarantee that change will bring new life into every area of your life you felt was dead or dying. You will see newness of life in your living arrangements, spiritual relationships, friendships, finances, family life, and more. I urge you to boldly stand strong in who you are and not be ashamed of who God has called you to be. It is time for you to proudly admit to yourself, as well as to everyone else you know, who you are and whose you are.

It took me almost losing everything to realize that God had always been with me, and even when I was deep in my sin, refusing to come to myself, he had been there with me all along. So the day I decided to make that first move to tell him yes, I never looked back and refuse to live in the guilt of who I used to be. I can attest to how God takes the sinner and separates them from the sin, cleaning them up and making them whole again. So the choice is yours this day, this moment, this very second. You have the option to continue running without knowing the dangers that lie ahead, or you could boldly decide to make a change for the better and give God the yes that he's been waiting for all along. For the words of an old hymnal still ring clearly in my ear, stating boldly and announcing to the world, "I have decided to follow Jesus, no turning back, no turning back."

CHAPTER 2

DEFEATING DISTRACTIONS

"Oh, be careful little ears what you hear, be careful little eyes what you see, be careful little tongue what you say, be careful little hands what you do..." It's funny how this old but simple Sunday school song still comes to my mind when I think about distractions and how we can defeat them. I recall we'd sing this song over and over on Sunday mornings, not knowing how the words of the song were proclaiming a warning to little children of the dangers of losing focus and sight of a true relationship with Christ. A relationship that involved true devotion and discipline. And we would sing and sing this song happily amongst each other, only to later learn how dangerous it is when we lose sight of the plan of God for our lives and let outside influences take over what we hear, see, speak, and even what we do.

The Bible clearly states a warning to all of us, decreeing, "Abstain from all appearance of evil" (1 Thessalonians 5:22), warning us that we should be weary of anything that could possibly take us from our rightful position as heirs to the throne. But the devil, with his cunning and deceptive self, just refuses to be defeated; he is determined to succeed at his plans of distracting us from gaining the ability to overcome all distractions. In addition he doesn't just know who we are but whose we are, and he, too, knows our weaknesses and strengths. It is his job and goal to knock us off our feet and our course with distractions, using any kind of plot, ploy, or scheme that will displace us from the move of God and safety of his arms. Which is why we must be careful of those distractions that could possibly affect what see, hear, say, and do. And I want you to know the words of that song still ring true today as it did when I sang it as a young boy, back in Sunday school.

Therefore it is so important to apply the words of this song to our lives every day. We must remain mindful of how what see, hear, say, touch, and where we go could possibly have a serious effect on our Christian lives and walk with God. And it is up to us to be cautious and always abounding in prayer to help remain on track and in rightful standing with our heavenly father. Be careful, saints. I cannot emphasize just how important it is for us to be alert and be careful of him who is seeking whom he can destroy.

I myself wish I had more carefully applied the words of that song to my life as a young man. If only I had paid more attention to where I went and the activities I participated in, then maybe, just maybe, I would have never been so distracted and could have seen the enemy's plot all along. You see, what you need to understand is that Satan doesn't give up easily and will continue to compose plans to distract and lure you away from God's predestined will for your life. He sends distractions that target you specifically, hoping he can change your destiny. I look back now and realize how great a mistake I made, having to face the truth and admit I foolishly let a distraction sent from the enemy send me into incarceration.

Am I Ready Now?

Grandmother always warned me about the company I kept and be mindful of who I chose to hang around. She always said how the company you keep should be a reflection of who you are, and more importantly who you desire to be. But I refused to listen to her, allowing the devil prime opportunity to distract me. So it started simply with the rage and bitterness I began to feel, which spiraled me into a rebellious state. I took on a new attitude and disposition, becoming someone my family could not recognize. I became too big and too bad to heed the warnings Grandmother would give with love and instead settled into a new crowd of friends. How many realize that the devil knows how to distract you? It is easier than you think. How many know that what ails you can become an attractant to others with similar traits and qualities? I had some hidden anger still residing in me from the death of my parents and was refusing to let the bitterness go as I blamed God for taking them away from me at such an early age. So I started hanging out with the wrong crowd.

See, I met some friends who were also angry and some just plain disobedient. We knew we were bad and so we took on a lifestyle of the streets. I found myself in the company of those known to have fierce behaviors and mannerisms that reflected negative lifestyles. I was hanging on the street corners past midnight before retreating to go home, and I soon began to take on the dispositions and perceptions of those with whom I hung around. One night while I was coming from church, I found myself engaged in the wrong company because the devil had a hit out on me. And me being foolishly ignorant to that planned "hit" got caught in the wrong place at the wrong time, when a brawl erupted over words. And as a result it landed me into a state of incarceration; through this I learned life and death were in the power of the tongue, because the company I insisted in keeping kept reacting upon something that had been said. I let the influential distractions of those around me drag me into a place where I felt trapped and unsure of what to do.

It was a difficult time for me as I stood before the judge, afraid and nervous at the same time, but I let a distraction pull me away from who God wanted me to be. And would you believe, the ones I was with denied having association with me as I was sentenced to incarceration? The time spent locked behind bars was a time of development and maturation, where I could only rely on myself. But even while I was there, strange but true, God allowed my gifts to shine and help others who were incarnated alongside me. I felt alone, stressed, and frustrated because I allowed foolish distractions to push me from my promise. I found myself feeling like Jonah trapped in the belly of the huge fish. It was not until I, like Jonah, came to a place of submission that out of nowhere my release came. But I did not say good-bye to my promise at that point; instead I said hello. Don't let distractions take you to a place you don't want to go.

Distractions can become a hindrance that obstructs one's focus in completing or accomplishing tasks, whether specified or not. Distractions are or can be:

- Annoying
- Trying
- Frustrating
- Irritating
- Consuming
- Disappointing
- Stressful
- Unscheduled

Some distractions can be small and some can be large, but when they come they become a hindrance and a road block, stopping us dead in our tracks. And we have had some things in our lives that have taken some, if not all, of our attention away from a primary task. I personally believe distractions are sent as tests of faith, endurance, patience, and, yes, even our ability to continue without throwing in the towel. They could possibly be a confirmation that God, too, has a sense of humor, but there comes a time when distractions get in the way and the choice is left to us as to what we want to do.

Distractions do not just come from one source. They surface during daily life events, such as a baby crying while you are trying to study for school and you must learn to balance study time as well as parenthood. For in the scripture we are taught that "To every thing there is a season, and a time to every purpose under the heaven" (Ecclesiastes 3:1). Therefore as we walk through this journey called life we will face unexpected distractions that happen seasonally as we mature and grow. There will be times when distractions will occur in your life, and the ones that come daily from life cannot always be prevented. And then there are some distractions which come that you can prevent by using preparation, planning properly, and being aware of your current life status. But, dear children, there are also some distractions that are heaven sent from your father above. You may be asking what I mean. What kind of distractions are heavenly sent? The scripture plainly states in Romans 8:28: " And we know that all things work together for good to them that love God." If we talk to Jairus, he may tell us that he and Jesus were on their way to his house to heal his ill daughter when a distraction made its way to Jesus. Do you remember the woman with the issue of blood? She was a distraction, but everything worked out for her good, and at the same time Jairus's, too.

For God demonstrated on that day faith was the key to receive healing, not one's wealth, status, or title. It should be noted not all godly sent distractions are for your good but used as a tool by God for ministry purposes, to do his will, and even to get your attention. If Job could testify to you today, his distraction was a test of faith and endurance by God to demonstrate how stronly he trusted God. And as each level of trial got even more difficult he remained ever faithful, never doubting, and speaking well of God. Be careful and know that God has the final say, and when he sends a distraction your way there is always a reasoning behind it.

But the most serious distractions that are sent come from Satan himself. It clearly states in the word that one needs to "Be sober, be vigilant; because your adversary the devil, as a roaring lion, walketh about, seeking whom he may devour" (1 Peter 5:8). Thus he has the power to use trickery, deception, lies, schemes, and other false tactics to pull you from the grace of God. It is his goal to confuse the saints of God and have us in a place of disillusion, disbelief, and doubt. He uses you for target practice, bringing distractions and detours to dissuade, trouble, and shake your faith. It is his goal to distract the very elect of God with whatever tactic his evil defense army chooses to use to cause you to fall. And I should let you know that, yes, he knows your weaknesses, secret desires, and wants. This is why you can be diligently persevering and serving in ministry and all of a sudden you find yourself tempted by a new convert who comes into the flock. See, he knows what you like and how to present something in front of you that catches your attention. Another prime example for some fellow believers who may not believe the devil sends distractions, is have you ever gotten a call from a former lover, boyfriend, or girlfriend? They claim to be just checking in on you but eventually the conversation moves from life to memories of sexual escapades and your previous sexual interactions. I don't know about you, but I have been there and it is a distraction that is difficult to overcome without realizing going backward profits you no progress. See, Satan is good at his job and he knows how to get you to a place where you find yourself questioning God, your faith, and what your next move should be. Just ask Eve, he got to her, and in turn he got to man, thus succeeding in distracting all mankind from their rightful place in God.

So you might be questioning just what in the world are the purposes for distractions in your life. Or why one must endure distractions. Simply put, one scripture comes to my mind: "...*when* he hath tried me, I shall come forth as gold" (Job 23:10). You see, defeating distractions all starts with understanding the exact purpose of them. They have been created for the testing of your faith. No one can overcome a distraction if they lack the faith of a mustard seed. Running from distractions will only make them return stronger, but your faith defeats their purpose, so I advise you to stand strong and stand in faith. I myself have had to endure distractions that have caused me to question God, but it is in talking with him in prayer I learned that faith is all I need, for without it I'm a sinking ship. They strengthen your faith to help you to learn to lean on God and trust him even when you cannot see him.

Distractions not only serve a purpose, but it is important to know that there are three different kinds of distractions one faces in life: spiritual, mental, and physical. When we speak of spiritual distractions these are those hindrances that take our attention away from our relationship with God, cause us to sin, bring about disobedience, involve temptation, and the trying of our faith. Spiritual distractions are ones that can be difficult to defeat and really try our faith. They ensue a battle between the spirit and the flesh to determine supremacy and can take one's focus and total attention from their personal walk and faith. The real challenge is letting faith lead you as you navigate through these interruptions that those in the world may not understand or see physically. In order to defeat these kinds of distractions one must know the word, as it is the tool to win the battle. Mental distractions are ones that deal with internal and external feelings, emotions, thoughts, disappointments, letdowns, and so on. Mental distractions are mental terrorists that take our minds hostage and invade our thoughts, troubling our world as we presently know it. Mental distractions can eventually seep into our spirits, thus causing deeper trouble as they destroy us mentally and physically, costing us great time lost and seeking real deliverance from outside sources. Distractions that deal with the physical sense involve sickness, ailments, human interaction, relationships, places, things, and people. These are those distractions to which we sometimes become unaware that can be controlled by our own actions and ceased immediately. But these are also those distractions that may possibly form strong emotional bonds that could damage our mental and spiritual perspective.

Principle #2
You've Got to Come to Yourself!

Once you've been called and have ceased running from your call, distractions will come and go. But what is important for your walk as you continue to press your way is to realize that in order to admit you are ready to press on, you need to come to yourself. How can one do this? Simply put, one needs to master the art of defeating distractions that come upon your life—whether they are sent by God, life, or

Satan—and then be able to navigate your way through the three kinds of distractions. In the Bible we see stories of those who have had problems when it comes to defeating the distractions within their lives. And there is none other who I can relate to more than Brother Sampson. He was a man who had strength, anointing, and the favor of the Lord upon his life, yet he still did not know how to totally defeat what distracted him until he decided that he needed to come to himself.

One of the hardest tasks to do when working in the will of God is learning how to not just avoid distractions that surface, but mastering how to overcome and defeat the distractions that transpire in your life. At a young age Sampson was walking in his calling and serving God with all of his heart. You see, he was destined for greatness as declared by the angel who informed his parents of his pending birth. It was immediate that he should be set aside, and because of the calling on his life he was set apart for greatness. And, yes, God has a call for all of us, but when distractions come into your life, how do you handle them? Are you able to ignore and continue or are you guilty of surrendering to the distractions that continue to plague your walk of faith? For me I was like Sampson in that I, too, knew I was anointed and I, too, knew God had a call upon my life, but as distractions came and went I did not know how to ignore them. It got to a point where I began to forget who I was and who I belonged to. But I was bound to spiritual temptations along with physical temptations that caused me to lose sight of the prize and my calling in Christ, yet not so difficult to beat as my environment. The scriptures tell us we should be set apart, but I let emotions and misunderstandings rage on and grow into frustrations that could not be controlled. I let myself rage from mental distractions that brought memories of pain and anger from the passing of my mother and father. I began to detest family, and as I mentally digressed so did I spiritually. I let anger reside within me spiritually, physically, and emotionally, taking over my thoughts and becoming a distraction that held me back from progressing.

You see, Sampson was a mighty man, but he had some issues. One, of course, was anger, another was trickery, and the other was the ability to let distractions take him from his rightful place in God. Have you found yourself giving in to the distractions that cause you to act out of your personality and character? What has had you so distracted that you cannot focus on serving God and abiding in his will completely? For Sampson he let anger prevail no matter how many battles he won and enemies he defeated. He could not remain calm, nor could he remain focused. One of the first keys to defeating distractions is being able to control one's emotions enough that you can see clearly. You have to be able to come to yourself enough to gather your emotions and get a clear view before reacting abruptly or unreasonably.

The second step one must accomplish is to come to the reality that trickery and games lead to confusion and distractions that bring about misconceptions and unclear decisions. One cannot allow distractions to overtake thought processes to the point you find yourself unclear and unsure of your next move. Distractions do come to hinder your progress, but remember you are more than a conqueror, so you must be able to defeat the mental games that one's mind can play. You are to let this mind, which is in Christ, be in you. He renews your mind daily. Sampson's problem was simple; he allowed all his thought processes become distracted through emotional baggage and foolery. As I recall my own personal life's journey, I must admit it is very difficult to mature to the point of life that you can admit the mistakes that cost you setbacks and challenges. I let the distractions of peers and the games they played to move me out of my position, pushing me to the point where I fell out of the grace of God, like Sampson, and was left standing looking a fool. One should never let the distractions of life take you from progression to digression.

One of the last tragedy's that took Sampson to a place he found hard to recover from was the ability to be so easily distracted. If Sampson had learned the first time from his first wife he would have never lost sight of the prize set before him, doing the permissible will of God. But Sampson let himself become so distracted that he lost sight of his purpose. At a stage like this God will bring you from a high place and set you in a low place of humility and obedience. Causing one to reconsider their mistakes and where they found themselves in error. In Sampson's case it took him to lose his actual sight and become imprisoned, then he realized it was time to come to himself. He had become so distracted it cost him his vision to progress, losing everything he had, but if you notice within the story his hair began to regrow. The regrowth of his hair showed he reached a level of maturity where he let all his past behaviors of trickery, anger, and being easily distracted to disappear and he took on maturity boldly. Sometimes it takes one to lose sight of where they are to come to a place of maturity. And Sampson's place of maturity led to him to being able to come to himself and defeat the enemy once and for all. In order for you, like myself, to graduate to the place where you can defeat the enemy, you must be able to come to yourself. When you come to yourself growth can take place, and where there is growth there is also maturity. I was able to come to myself and mature once I could admit my feelings, pushing past how I felt, negative distractive actions, and following Christ wholeheartedly.

For, saints, we need to come to a place where we can mature and grow in faith, so we can defeat distractions that come our way.

Remember, to defeat distractions it is going to take faith. For without faith it is impossible to please God. Don't let fear and the distractions that come from life push you into place you cannot mature or grow. It is through growth and maturity you can successfully come to yourself and declare victory in Jesus' name.

CHAPTER 3

IDENTIFYING COUNTERFEIT AND AUTHENTIC

Do you know who you are? Do you really know who you are in Christ? So often when it comes to our identity in Christ we seem to neglect to inform others who we truly are and whose we are. Is it possible we are ashamed to reveal our true born-again identities? Or are we sure we really know who we are?

There are going to be times in your faith when you walk this road that you may find yourself questioning who you are and if you are really a child of the most-high king, but let me make this clear. As a matter of fact let me make this very clear: never allow anyone to question your identity. Always know who you are, and always be certain you know who you are. God, our heavenly father, is looking for followers who are not just reassured in knowing who they are and whose they are, but can identify the real saints from the "aint's," as I like to call them.

Do you remember the familiar Bible story of Cain and Abel? More specifically, do you remember when God was searching for Abel and Cain would not reveal to God where his brother was? But the truth of the matter was Cain had slain his own brother out of jealousy and anger. To me it is a story that reveals how God can identify those who are authentic, genuine, sold-out, for-real Christians from the so-called fakers, game players, and the ones who claim to be "saved" but when the truth is revealed they are not at all who they appear or claim to be. And, saints, there comes a time when you have to demonstrate to God who you really are. Are you really the person who prays all night, or seeks his face? Do you really read your word, or better yet are you who you say you are? Have you taken the title but refused the assignment and all the tasks it truly entails? Or are you a fake and a fraud who has the main goal to be seen?

When Jesus told us to take up his cross and follow him, little did some know that meant we were picking up the work, toil, labor where he left off. You cannot truly claim to be saved and not be a worker in his vineyard. God knows his fruit and he knows whom he has called, chosen, and, yes, selected to do his ultimate will. But are you ready for the task at hand? You can tell me how you've decided to answer his call, avoid and yield the temptations of distractions, but are you ready to be totally honest and demonstrate true authenticity? I ask, how real are you, my sister? How real are you, my brother? Yes, you can talk the talk, walk the walk, sing the songs, give till it hurts, but are you truly who you say you are? It's one thing to lie to yourself but it's another to lie to God, assuming he'll believe anything you are saying. Real, authentic saints do not wait for crowds, they show up in good and bad weather, and they are humbly submissive, eager, and willing to work, but most of all they are all in no doubt about it. But for those of you who are "claiming" to be what you truly are not. I warn you God is not a fool. He can see beyond your fake and phoniness. If you are willing to sacrifice and submit to the greater cause for God's glory and magnification, then you know you're ready for next-level ministry and promotion. But if you cannot even give a ride to the saint you see walking to the bus stop, I think you need to rethink and re-evaluate who you are.

This walk we are walking, I think so many saints forget it is not your walk but a journey assigned from on high that expects you to work and be real. God cannot use fake, unrealistic, fictional people who neglect to do what they need to do to please God and get his message across the globe. When it comes to Christianity, when it comes to serving God, one must remember we have a task at hand, and that is to win souls for Christ. But how can one win souls if you have never given your soul to Christ? One of the keys we have to remember as saints of God is authenticity gets God's attention. God is not one for copying; he likes originality. As a Christian originality is what gets you to that next level of praise, to the next-level ministry. It gets you through to the next level of service for kingdom building. We all have been given gifts that when used collaboratively exhort God and promote his powerful kingdom. One of the hardest things we can do and learn from Christ is to remember that authenticity; our sense of originality is what makes us who we are, and it is important to know who we are in Christ. This is because once we know who we are in Christ, then we know who Christ is and we know what Christ did for us. Thus we know why we work for Christ. We cannot let the devil play tricks in our minds and heads allowing us to think our service unto God, is nothing more but busy work.

Kingdom-mindedness is the key to access entrance into God's Kingdom. When I think back to when I first entered ministry, I was eager, I was excited, I was glad. Yet what I learned was it's not so much what I do when it comes to serving Christ, but it is how I do what I do.

- Do you do you serve with a smile or a frown?
- Do you have a nasty disposition?
- Can you take correction without getting angry?
- Can you obey leadership and follow directions?
- Are you willing to serve wholeheartedly?
- Are you willing to give tithes, seeds, and offerings?
- Are you willing to sacrifice?
- Can you really give it your all without realizing that there is a greater price to pay?

People need to realize one thing in life, and that is without your story there is no glory! Everyone's story is different. Your story depicts who you are in Christ. I know one of the hardest things for me to do in ministry was to be submissive, because being submissive meant I couldn't be in charge and I had to follow someone else's directions. I had to listen. I had to say, "Yes, ma'am" or "No, sir." I had to do what I was told, and I could not say anything otherwise, but in the long run it was all working together for my good because it was in that training that I learned how to be a better Christian. When we think about authenticity it's all about taking our originality and who we are and using them for the betterment and service for God. God's not looking for the cookie-cutter-shaped Christian in this generation, but he is looking for the Christian who is willing to say, "Here I am, God. Do you want me to go to the mountains and preach your gospel? Do you want me to go feed the hungry on the street? God, I don't have but $2, yet I'm willing to give that to the sister so she can get on the bus." God is no longer looking for you to be looking at who's looking at you, but instead he's looking for the ones who are looking to do what he has called them to do.

This is a new age, a new era in a new generation, and we must remember that with each generation the world gets wickeder and wickeder, and as the world gives in to the wiles of the devil we need to be even more determined to serve God and do his will. We've got to become submissive and be eager to do whatever he asks of us, but God does not need saints who are unwilling to give their all. Have you forgotten God sent his son? His only begotten son Christ gave his own life on the cross for us, therefore you must remember: "For to me to live is Christ, and to die is gain…" (Philippians 1:21).

Simply put, the scripture means it is more to live, to suffer is Christ, to go through is Christ, to endure hardship as a good solider is Christ, to have setbacks, disappointments, and even failures are Christ. But, beloved, to die is to gain meaning to gain your crown, to gain your robe, to gain peace in the midst of storms, to gain a sense of accomplishment, and winning souls for Christ is gain. No man can gain anything if you're not willing to lay down selfishness, greed, envy, and laziness—and, yes, you must have dedication, too. Now is the time to do all that you can do. I want people to realize it is not easy serving God, but what I will tell you is that I still look back and I wonder how I have made it this far. When I first started in ministry I wasn't willing to give my all to God. When I first started ministry I wanted things to be about me. I wanted things to be my way, but now I look back and I laugh at that little boy. I laugh at how immature I was. Now I've grown to a level of maturity that has put me above the mind-set of "me" and into the mind-set of serving. I never knew fully what it took to serve God, but I now know what it takes to give God all of me. I now know what it's like to surrender to God, and I know more than anything in this world that I am sold out for Christ.

We have to remember that in order for us to gain victory in any adversity, we have to be real with ourselves and question what we are doing wrong. We talked about the call of Christ and answering the call. Yes, we talked about avoiding distractions and the temptation of distractions standing in our way. We've even gone as far as to discuss defeating distractions, but now we need to talk about authenticity versus us being real or counterfeit for God.

Principle #3
Honesty Is the Best Policy!

How can you be ready for the call and purpose of God for your life when you're not true to who you are and who God called you to be?

- No deacon can be the preacher.
- No preacher can be the usher.
- No usher can be the janitor.
- No janitor can be the choir director.
- No choir director can be the soundman.
- No soundman can be the parking lot attendant.

You see, everybody has a distinct calling and a distinct placement in ministry, but the interference and the discrepancy come when we would rather not be who we are called to be and instead show no originality and just be counterfeit. God hates it when we're not ourselves, so why boldly proclaim ourselves to be something that we're not? We've gotten to the point of ministry now where there are people claiming that they are tele-evangelists, preachers, missionaries, and such. I asked you in the beginning of this chapter, do you know who you are, and do you know whose you are? Because if you know who you are then you know whose you are. And knowing who you are you, who you serve, and what you been called to do as well as where you belong in ministry are important.

Ministry is something that you cannot do overnight. It takes time, years of dedication, and it takes you to fully be able to surrender and submit to the mission. Which is why one of the first keys when it comes to authenticity is submission. You have to be submissive to God and his will. When you look at the story of Cain and Abel, you might be questioning why use Cain and Abel for this story, as it looks more usable when it comes to brotherhood and unity, but when I see this story I think of ministry and how honesty is the best policy.

So often ministries become destroyed, torn down, and pastors or preachers or ministers of the gospel become discouraged because when they get to a certain level and look around, they get the Cain spirit. This is a time or period where frustration and anger, as well other influenctual negative spirits, take reign and rule over one's mind and life. Where they once were hardworking and willing to do ministry enthusiastically without complaining and murmuring, now the problem is that there's a clash in the present day, beloved. This is a significant clash in the ministry of God, and it's amongst the men and women who proclaim his gospel. When it comes to honesty we have to realize that there's no need to be jealous of this person or that person, because the Bible speaks about seasons of time. And it doesn't just speak about seasons. We must realize that sometimes God places us in a position because of a condition, and he knows that we may not be able to handle a 10,000-people ministry but we can handle a ten-people ministry and run it well. But the trouble comes in our minds when we let the devil give us distractions, where we suddenly find ourselves questioning our call. Or we find ourselves becoming counterfeit brothers and sisters of the gospel because we lose sight of the greater race and purpose for us being here. I ask you, don't be counterfeit when it comes to ministry and doing the work of the Lord.

Looking at the story of Cain and Abel we see two brothers who were the sons of Adam and Eve, the first man and woman on earth. They were two children they had been blessed with, but the problem came when one refused to give of his best to the Lord as an offering. He was selfish, not genuine, nor authentic, while the other gently tended to the flocks and gave God of his best and put his heart into everything he did with excellency. So I ask you today, which one of the two are you? Are you Cain who was jealous, in a place where you are not giving your all and your best in serving God, a place where God finds that you are being counterfeit instead of being authentic while working in the ministry? Or are you like Abel, somebody who's willing to get out there and work, someone who's willing to give your best and your all to the savior regardless of what everything looks like, seems like, or may be? So who are you?

For a long time I wondered, questioned, and looked at this story, and from this story one of the first things you need to know is that honesty is the best policy. You have to be honest when it comes to ministry and working in ministry. It is not something that can be accomplished without honesty. You have to be honest with who you are and in knowing what you're called to do. It is essential you be honest and know how your serving God will benefit others. As a pastor for many years I've always wondered, and I've looked. I am not ashamed to admit I've looked at other ministries and how these ministries flourished and blossomed. But when I looked at my own it appeared like it was not going anywhere. I had friends in the gospel who would invite me to their churches to fellowship, and I'd see how they moved into these grandiose sanctuaries. I never got jealous, but it pushed me to work harder and stay focused. They would show off to me all the newly acquired land, new fellowship halls, and how they had all these parking lots. And faithful me I was still in a small business park where our sanctuary doubled as the fellowship hall, my associate pastor's office was also used as the kitchen, my office was the second emergency exit, and we only had one of each bathroom. Although we had central air conditioning, when it got hot we would turn on large industrial fans open the doors and have service with the door wide open, not ashamed of giving God the praise, but I kept consistent.

Like Abel in the scriptures I stayed confident, remembering and meditating upon the thought, "Now unto him that is able to do exceeding abundantly above all that we ask or think, according to the power that worketh in us" (Ephesians 3:20). I did not know what God had for me when it came to ministry renovations and elevations, but I rejoiced gladly for all those who showed up and showed me what God did for them. And instead of me questioning about God, "Why not me? Why not my ministry?" I blessed God for them and their successes. But would you believe that in time, lo and behold, doors started to open for my own ministry? Miracles, signs, and wonders began to manifest within my own ministry as God graduated us and elevated us into a new edifice. I laugh now, but as I reflect on the process I'm glad I waited for the Lord to keep his promise. My sincerity and faithfulness paid off so much because God opened the door and we were able to walk through the door. As I think and look back now I also laugh, because some of my fellow sisters and brothers of the gospel who were so big and bold and proclaimed this and that of what God did for them now have nothing. Some of them aren't even pastoring anymore, some of them lost those super large and grand ministries they had, others have been reduced in size, or don't have them anymore. But I look out every Sunday, every Tuesday-night service, and other services as we gather. I look at my flock and realize in my faithfulness to God I like Abel tended to the flock faithfully. I kept believing and speaking the word, I kept in prayer, I stayed consistent in giving tithes, seeds, and offerings. Truth be told although some of my members and officials could see it, there were other who could not, but I had a vision, and I was determined to see it come to pass. I remained faithful in giving and sowing my love, my joy, my peace, my faithfulness. Yes, all for the work of the gospel so that people might be saved in his name and proclaim his will so that they, too, might become fishers of men.

Saints, I want you to understand and realize that honesty, when it comes to God, never, never, never lets you down. Because when you're honest with God, he can trust you with anything and everything. And when God trusts you it is an honor and should be considered just how special you are to him and how much you mean to him. True authenticity is to be trustworthy, honest, open, aware, and trusting of who you are, whose you are, and knowing his will for your life. And he has trusted me with a ministry that has grown as I started from the bottom, but now I am further than where I've been and where I could only imagine going. I know God still has more in store for me and it's just the process I have to undertake as one of the keys to gaining eternal kingdom-hood. It is time we realize there's a process to doing everything. Ask yourself, did Cain put his best foot forward with God and got what he truly deserved by not serving with gladness in spite of all the vain work he did? He would've had no need to be jealous of a brother who was willing and open to being genuine and himself in devoting his whole energy and heart into serving God authentically. For you see, Abel was a man who was authentic, and his brother Cain was a counterfeit who only looked the part but could not fill the role. Or are you like Abel, willing and able-minded and spirited to do all that is possible when it comes to serving Christ?

So today I urge you, brothers and sisters, don't let the Cain spirit overtake you or you'll find yourself starting to take on a spirit of fraudulent irrationalism that may not be worth it, or it can cost you your soul and everything that makes you whole. For you see, Cain was sent away far from the presence of God, left only with a mark of identification to keep him from any kind of ostracizing and harm. Whereas in all reality he was already set apart and isolated from the godly right he could have inherited if he had only been authentic with God by showering him with honor, devotion, and love. For once one is overtaken by this counterfeit spirit, everything you view is never really what you think, what you see, what you thought you knew, and who you think you are in a sense. You must press past all that with a strong sense of determination and allow him to see who you are. Today God is looking for:

- Authentic praisers
- Authentic worshippers
- Authentic servants
- Authentic vineyard workers
- Authentic ministers
- Authentic preachers
- Authentic evangelists
- Authentic deacons

- Authentic teachers of the gospel
- Authentic saints rightly dividing and declaring the gospel

They are going to have the same mind-set and be able as well as willing to say, "I'm going to be honest with you, God. I only have this one fruit, but it's my best and you deserve it." Make the time today and boldly declare with all openness, "I had struggles. I've had problems. But, God, to you be all glory! I'm going to be honest with you God. My brother may be fruitful in this and that, but I am still here and you've been faithful to me." So take a lesson from Cain and Abel and learn from it, understanding that ministry is not so much about what you get as what you gain. Beloved, gaining takes precedence over getting, because when you gain things God can trust you with things. And as you gain, you learn; as you learn, you grow to trust in God even more through faithfulness and your fruitfulness. Remember you are in the faithfulness of God, you are the favor of God, and you are truly blessed and highly favored. When you look at yourself never be too ashamed to declare as I do on a daily basis, "I really don't know where I would be without the Lord on my side. I really do not know where I would be if I had gotten the Cain spirit and became disappointed, distracted, and destitute!" But, glory to God, we are safe in his arms and we are real, open, obedient to become who he has created and destined for us to become. To God be the glory!

CHAPTER 4

MESSAGE FROM THE MESS

In the words of a song, I ask you today, is there anything too hard for the Lord? And I've come to declare to you, you, and yes even you—no! Nothing is ever impossible for God to solve and to do. He clearly asks in his word, "...is there any thing too hard for me?" (Jeremiah 32:27). So knowing this in every situation you've faced or encountered, maybe it is time to rethink these obstacles and consider God is sending you messages in every mess you encounter. Have you ever been in a mess? I'm talking about a real mess where you cannot seem to recover or even get a grip of the situation at hand. The mess becomes so messy that you find yourself tumbling out of control without the ability to regain composure or even get a grip on the situation. You begin to succumb to the situation itself instead of leaning on what you know and what you "claim" to believe. It gets to the point where you start to question God, asking him those six favorite "W" questions:

- Who can help me?
- What did I do to deserve this?
- When can I escape this?
- Where are you, God?
- Why is this happening to me?
- Why God, am I in this place?

And out of exaggerated frustrations your joy turns to sorrow, your smile into a frown, and your faith into disbelief. But this is the time when you need to start declaring and decreeing, "Whatever God is trying to do to get my attention, I'm listening with ears wide open, so speak, Lord, speak!"

In our lives today messes come whether situational, intentional, or even unexpected. But how you react to these messes is what sets you apart from the rest of the world. One of the hardest messes I had to recover from was my near-fatal car accident in 2004. I found myself crashing head first into a building marquee. I was driving from a worship service feeling extremely tired but determined to make it to my final destination. I remember getting into my car but not getting out. I was driving around the streets of Baltimore City, and from what I recall I had just went through a green light. I sped up some to attempt to keep up with traffic but probably was a little too heavy on the gas. As I kept going I recall my eyes getting cloudy, and the next thing I knew someone was knocking on my car window.

I did not understand what was going on, but I noticed I was in a lot of pain and very uncomfortable. When I was able to focus my eyes finally I went to rub my head and noticed a liquid dripping; unbeknownst to me it was blood. I tried to turn my head but could not, nor could I move my body. Confused, dazed, and drowsy I realized I was still in my car but could not for the life of me figure out what was going on. It was not until a paramedic came to the car and started to speak to me slowly and explain what exactly was going on. I was told I had had an accident and they were preparing to use the jaws of life to cut me out of the car. Due to the immediate impact of my car slamming into the marque, I was rushed to the University of Maryland's shock trauma center, where it was discovered my brain was hemorrhaging. To control the bleeding I was placed on the bed vertically for a week to assist in my brain healing. Aside from the brain bleeding, I suffered some minor injuries as well. But thanks be to God! Would you believe in three days the hemorrhaging ceased and I was made whole? He is not just a Jehovah-Rapha, my healer, but I can testify he knows how to look beyond your faults to see your needs and clean up the mess you made!

As I tell this story I am still amazed at how God was able to pull me from my mess and push me into the call he had for my life. I was diagnosed with severe sleep apnea and doctors thought it best I did not drive for the next six months to keep me under observation. Apparently I had fallen asleep at the wheel and lost control of my car. Today I proclaim I am totally cured of sleep apnea and can drive myself around without any assistance from anyone else. Some may question what's the message I learned from my mess was. For me the message was simple and clear: God was getting my attention, so he could bring my mind under subjection. I had begun to lose focus on my call and the work I was sent to do. He needed me to remain devoted and faithful in ministry and stop "falling asleep" on my job. It was time for me to cease slacking and actually get to work with all my heart, mind, and soul, ready to do the will of Christ. When you fully devote yourself to accepting God's call, then you can avoid the messes that deter you from success.

Yes, it is understandable that when situations or "messes" come we get frustrated, distracted, act out of character, and so on. But have you thought that maybe in this mess God is trying to send you a message? You see, God will send situations and challenging events in your life, but as a method to get your attention. And once he has your full attention it is then that he can use the mess to provide a message to you, whether of ministry, encouragement, or even to discipline. The choice is up to you. Whether you are willing to receive or refuse, you have a choice. But I should make you aware that God's got a message for you in all the mess. How willing are you to receive his message? Ask yourself:

- Do I want to be free from those things that have me bound?
- Do I want to advance in kingdom-hood?
- Am I ready to stop falling into "messes" and "pitfalls" that have me bound?

When listening for the voice of God it is not so much how loud the volume may be as to what exactly is being said and how it is said. Yes, God does speak to each and everyone one of us through his holy spirit, but he also speaks even more clearly through his word. I know there have been some that make you feel God has this big, spooky voice that may frighten you or scare you, but he speaks softly, sweetly, and clearly if you listen closely. All you have to do is read his word. Don't you know his word is "a lamp unto my feet, and a light unto my path" (Psalms 119:105)? When God desires to talk to you he does so through his word, so it is essential that you stay focused and devote yourself to reading and studying the word of God. Yes, prayer is a key when forming a relationship with God and communicating with him on a daily basis, but his word is the second piece that seals the relationship-communication contract.

When God speaks he wants or yearns to give you guidance and lessons in life that will keep you focused and persevering. And for God to get your attention sometimes he uses the "mess" to send a message. What is important for you to realize is that when the mess appears, take the time to ask God, "What is the message you want me to get? God, what is it you want me to learn, or to change, or even to understand more clearly?" You see, some of the messes we fall into are of our own doing, whether through disobedience, pride, selfishness, anger, envy, strife, and so on. Instead of focusing on how to immediately get out of the mess, take the time to form a stronger communication relationship with God, and through seeking him inquire about the message he has for you. It may seem easy, but to let you know sometimes God does not answer immediately. At other times he wants you to learn a lesson before you understand and get the message from the mess.

Reflecting back on my own life I can recall specific moments, instances, and times when the message from my mess sent me spiraling into a maze of confusion and unassured reasoning. I would cry and whine to God, asking him if he was sure he wanted me to teach me this, warn the people about that, or proclaim exactly what I heard. I would question his way, will, and desire for me, refusing to listen and believing I knew what was best for me than he did. But what I came to learn is that God has a way that you can't go under or avoid. Expect the unexpected. See, we can say and plead those fake and phony cries. "God, I will do your will if you just let me have this" or "God, I see what you mean but if you give me a second chance I promise…" Are you kidding yourself? Do you really hear yourself trying to plea and bargain with God? Do you know who he is? Do you really know who he is? He is the Alpha and the Omega, the beginning and the end. He is the good shepherd, our bright and morning star, and he is God. He knows you and me better than we do, and he knows our true heart, so playing the fake and ignorance game with God does not work.

What does work is God demonstrating to you how powerful he is and how he holds it all in his hands. God sends these "messes"—or as I like to call them, "pitfalls"—to get your attention and direct you back to him. I know life has been difficult, I know life has dealt you an unfair hand, I know life has not been at all what you expected or hoped it be. But I am here to assure you and remind you that things get easier when you heed his message, and he in turn will deliver you from the "pitfall" or "pitfalls" (for those who needed more than one mess to get their attention) that you have fallen into and need rescuing from.

I found myself in more "pitfalls" than I could crawl out of because I did not get the messages from God, or better yet I chose to stay in my "mess" because I found more comfortability and familiarity in the dark place rather than I did in the light. Is that you, too? It took total deliverance and obedience for me to realize that if I listened to the voice of God, I could get out of my "pitfalls" or "messes" and be set free to live my life as a blessed and highly favored man of God.

By no means am I saying that God sent me to prison. I believe that we have a God who gives us the opportunity of freedom of choice, but within the choices that we make our consequences are the products of the decisions we make. Even though God did send me to prison he used me within the prison. I'm letting you know that there are some situations that we are engulfed in yet God still uses us in the mess that we make.

Maybe it is time for you to be free from the mess, so boldly decree, "I'm ready for my message!" And God seeing your heart will open his and tell you what he wants you to know to bring about a change. If you don't believe me, there is someone else you can ask: Joseph. If my testimony does not reach you, maybe his can. Let's look and review the significance and story of Joseph. Let's let him help you and me get the message God has for you.

What you need to remember is that:

- Part of your defeat is your environment
- Your environment prevents your deliverance
- It's time to come outside of that environment
- You don't release into those robbing your environment

Principle #4
Pitfalls Lead You to the Call!

Let's look at Brother Joseph and how his landing in a pitfall didn't just lead him to the call upon his life, but to receive the message God had for him. In the story of Joseph we learn how he was one who was highly favored by his father and cared for deeply. And just like him God cares for you and loves you, too. But the story gets intriguing when Joseph received a special present, a coat, from his father. But not using common sense he decided to run and show off this coat to his brothers, bragging about his new gift. One of the first things one needs to understand is that there are some instances when we get our own selves and others into a mess, we are put into uncomfortable circumstances orchestrated by God, where we lose control. We decide to go and do something irresponsibly, which befalls a hardship upon us before we can even see our way out. In Joseph's case he created a mess for himself by going and bragging about his gift from his father. This immature action brought him into a mess he could not dig himself out of.

From his irresponsible action his brothers conspired to do harm to him, but thanks to one brother speaking up they instead placed their brother inside a pit. And this is what happens to saints when we decide to act irresponsibly, because God sends us into a "pitfall" to catch our attention and see he has a message for us while in our mess. God did send grace Joseph's way through his brother's suggestion to spare his life, and you, too, have received the grace of God. But how many know that grace can run out? Thus it is up to you to either remain in a dark, cold place of misery (the pit) or come into the knowledge of accepting God's will for your life and listening to the message he wants to tell you. Are you willing to take the message from the mess, or remain in a place of darkness until you yield?

Yes, we can boldly declare and brag like Joseph about how we are favored, but we neglect to realize God has set a plot to put us in a position that results in an ultimatum. The choice he gives, like Joseph's brothers, is harm from our ignorance or to save our lives, but he places us in holding. And when we emerge from the deep pit that we were buried in, what we fail to realize is God did this to humble us. And he does it to free us from a reprobate mind and life of terrible sin for our disobedience. We should also be aware that submission to God is essential when we can no longer escape from our "messes" and "pitfalls" that God has placed us in. Freedom is only a "yes" away and all it takes is to seek the message he has for you and change your ways. Running profits you nothing but a repeatable cycle, until God gets tired and leaves you to figure out how to come back into his good graces. Not only do the "pitfalls" or "messes" he sends you into get your attention to listen to the message from God, but it does something else: it provides you with the direction for your life, his will and call.

One cannot accept the call of God if they are not meek. When you are humble God can work with you, shape you, and mold you into who he desires you to be. But when one is not, he cannot use you for his glory, nor will he get the glory from the works you will perform under his call. So often we get vain and puffed up, but he knows how to bring us down to a place of humility and servanthood. It is then that God can remove us from that spiritual timeout (the pit) and allow us to come to ourselves just enough to be rescued, positioned in a place of servitude. Remember Joseph was sold into slavery, and once we are set free from that pit God places us for his glory to do unto others. We know that as the story concludes Joseph who looked like he was set up for failure, in reality was set up to answer his call and heed the message from his mess. What is that message? "Seek ye the LORD while he may be found, call ye upon him while he is near" (Isaiah 55:6).

From this we learn first off that with saints God will sometimes place us in a position of surrender whether we want to be there or not. And learning from Joseph we see he landed in a place that he could not escape until God ordained it to happen. Acceptance of the call from God is a pivotal moment and giant step in our Christian walk. Those who choose to ignore his call, as I did, be forewarned: you just may end up like Joseph, stuck in a "pit," until he decides to set you free. And even if that still does not work you will keep finding yourself in pitfalls during your life until you fully and willfully surrender to his will. As for myself I found myself running and, yes, I was a Joseph, stuck in a pit, miserable and angry. I could not understand how a God who sat so high could let me be stuck in a place so low. But one thing we all must remember is that, "Nay, in all these things we are more than conquerors through him that loved us" (Romans 8:37).

So make the first step today to keep you falling from the grace of God by looking for the message in all of the mess. It is time to realize you are nothing without Christ, and on him and him alone do you stand strong. Today is your day to be free of any obstacles that will block your progress as you continue on this journey we call life.

Keep your mind made up and let ole' Satan know there is no stopping you now as you press toward the mark of the prize of the high calling, and learn that from every mistake you make God sends a message. Take that message to heart and know only someone who loves you more than you'll ever know will set you up for position, prosperity, and promise. All you have to do is allow him to lead you to the call. But beware of those unexpected yet necessary pitfalls, and remember that he will deliver you from them all.

CHAPTER 5

THE ACCEPTANCE OF GOD'S WILL

Naaman, where are you? Where are my Naamans at? Ah yes, Naaman, there you are. Are you a Naaman, sir? Or you, madam, are you a Naaman? Definitely you have got to be a Naaman. I can see it in your eyes. The worried look, the prominence radiating from your pores, the stance you take when walking, and, yes, that pride. Yes, that pride that announces to everyone you are someone important, someone who has a title, someone who is of high status, someone… someone like you. Are you sure you're not a Naaman? You look important, sound important, for God's sake you must be important, but do you really need to be that significant? Seriously this walk of life is not based upon a popularity contest or how much class you have. It's time to stop making the excuses and assuming you need so much to accept your calling and humbly walk into it graciously.

Or if you insist you can be a Naaman and say, "Lord I brought this with me, my diamonds, my car, my house, my I-Pad, my Rolex, a million dollars, and here I am. I'm ready for what you have for me." Can I just say this, beloved? It's time for you to get over your self-exaggerated, self-imagined, self-indulged, self-declared image of who you are and become who God desires you to be. The question is, can you deny the prideful spirit of Naaman long enough to let God do a mighty work through you and in you as well? Now is the time, for tomorrow is never promised, to come to yourself and let go of what was and look to what is, a prime opportunity to serve God, assuring his will is done and he gets the glory, not you.

Some of you, I know, may be asking, "Why in the world are you referring to me or anyone else as 'Naaman'?" But let me give you a refresher course in why I called you by that name specifically. Naaman was a man of prominence and promotion in the Old Testament who was large and in charge. He had everything one desires in life, such as:

- Wealth
- Status and class
- Honor
- Popularity
- Governmental favor
- A great job
- A beautiful spouse
- Servants
- A mansion

But as we continue to read the story in 2 Kings chapter 5, we learn he had an issue, and this issue he hid from everyone in the world, except from those who either resided with him or were close to him. So long story short, with the help of a servant girl he learned his issue could be resolved. He set out to do just that: find a resolution. But I should let you know that on the journey he decided to take everything that signified he was of high class and status. Yet when he arrived at the place of resolution he learned that title, status, and class were never needed in the first place to gain what he truly desired and wanted so badly. He had a huge spirit of pride that stood in the way of him gaining victory over his issue that had plagued him for so long. If it had not been for the words spoken to him by someone without title, class, or wealth, he would have still been in a place of frustration, disillusion, and entrapment for the rest of his days.

See, so often we create these "ideals" in our heads that in order to be worthy of God we must have this or we must have that. In reality he only requires of us a willing mind and a willing heart. I urge you to not be like Naaman or become a Naaman, where you are so caught up in what you have, your status, your class, and your title, and more, that you possibly miss the blessing God has specifically for you. My mistake in not accepting the call so openly was believing I had to be someone else and not myself. When I looked around in church all I saw were people who had titles, popularity, prideful attitudes, high social standing in the church, expensive clothing on, and some known as "well to-do" or just plain wealthy. I figured, why in the world would God need a man like me to proclaim his gospel when he's got those who have it all and more? I even questioned God over and over, asking him if he was sure he wanted a young man like myself. I let what I saw take over my mind and give me insecurities, believing one had to have all of this and all of that to be a minister of his gospel and serve him. This mind-set got so deep inside my head that I began to become ashamed of who Donnell was and started portraying myself as someone else. I even went as far as to take on a new persona, act differently amongst all I knew, purchase new clothing, and literally imitate all I had seen, not realizing I was falling down a dangerous path.

The path that like Naaman entered in, I started letting pride and my status hold me back from being who I really wanted and desired to be. And it left me feeling alone, confused, and unsure of what I wanted to do or who I wanted to be. I started believing I had to be more than who I was and, foolishly like Naaman, I almost let my issue overtake my chance for a resolution. I knew who I was called to be, and if not for the holy spirit whispering in my ear one night, ministering to me, I do not think I would be preaching today. And some of you reading this book right now know who you are and why God has created you, but you have let the ideals of the world, such as popularity, fame, and even fortune, mislead and push you away from fulfilling the will of God. But the scripture reminds us to "be ye stedfast, unmoveable, always abounding in the work of the Lord…" (1 Corinthians 15:58), which means we have got to be about the work of the one who has created us and declare his power to the world. It is not a time to be inconsistent in our beliefs and ministry. No longer should we let the ideals of the world push us out of our position and will of Christ. We must do the will of the one who has sent us here on earth and cry out to the world about salvation and the saving power of Jesus Christ.

Do you not realize that even in the Bible, God used anyone he could find to do his will? So that does not mean you get a break. In today's world we are so consumed with any and everything that we forsake the will of God and let him down. But use today as your first step in spiritual maturity by answering boldly without a flinch, "Yes, Lord, I accept your will for my life. And I will do the will of the one who has created me." For don't you know you have been created for so much more than what you could ever know?

Principle #5
God Has No Respect of Person!
(Status, Title Don't Matter!)

Whom God choses and whom he calls is his decision and not ours. He is sovereign, therefore he has the power to do as he pleases, how he pleases, and when he pleases. Thus I must reiterate we have no power over God and whom he chooses, uses, and calls to do his will. "Moreover whom he did predestinate, them he also called: and whom he called, them he also justified: and whom he justified, them he also glorified" (Romans 8:30). Therefore when he calls I suggest you answer him wholeheartedly, ready for the task at hand no matter what may lie ahead. He wants volunteers; he hasn't the time to take hostages. God does not look at titles, one's status, financial statements, or even educational background. He only looks at one thing: the mind, a willing mind. If anyone can testify to that, ask the former Saul of Tarsus, who we now know as the apostle Paul. Funny thing is he had a title, he had wealth, he had status, and, yes, the educational background, but God looked past everything and saw his mind. He saw a man with a mind of determination and said, "If he can move passionately to persecute my children, then I know he will have that same passion for doing my will," and so it happened. Do you realize the same happens to all of us when God takes a long, hard look at our minds? He sees the potential inside of each and everyone's mind and anticipates the great passion that will be put toward doing his will and serving him.

You see, Saul of Tarsus was a very powerful and known man of power who had an extensive record for persecuting followers of Christ. He was a man with a great passion to assure that the lives of the disciples and all those who followed Christ were made a living hell. This man put fear in the lives of all the believers and followers of Christ and proudly spoke against those who believed. But one day as he was traveling, he had an encounter that changed his life for the better. Who would believe God would take a man who fought against him and set him up to work for him? Isn't it funny how God's plans never line up with man's?

Saul was then converted immediately on the road from this encounter and changed in an instant for the better. Although he lost his sight, eventually he regained it, as well as a new take on who God is and his almighty power. No longer was he Saul but Paul, and from that moment on he became an avid apostle who boldly and unashamedly proclaimed the word of the Lord. You see, like Saul—or shall I say, Paul—God takes us through a process when he claims us as his own. And as we undergo his process changes occur for the better that sets us on a course for greatness and preparation to do the will of God. He takes us from a place of uncertainty and darkness, and leads us, like Paul, into the marvelous light.

As in Saul's case he was called, and God took him through a process of rebirth and renewal that developed him into a lethal weapon for Christ, determined to do the will of the one who sent him. And we, too, are like Paul, being taken through a transitional stage of rebirth and renewal as he prepares us to take on the call he has for us. It is a stage of preparation and training, so therefore those who run from the call, you may not realize, but God has already equipped you for the work at hand like Paul. As a matter of fact he has removed the scales off your eyes to provide you with new sight for your assignment. The new sight allows you to see past your own fear and the looks of others to continue boldly with a brand-new outlook on the mission God has called you to do. Remember to use your new sight and perspective to keep yourself focused on the duty at hand as you, "Look unto Jesus the author and finisher of our faith" (Hebrews 12:2). And with his help you can prevail, but it is essential for you to not just answer the call, but submit. For some the idea of submitting seems frightening, but when you come to yourself you realize there is so much more worth fighting for when it comes to serving God and obeying his will.

In addition I want you to understand that no matter who you claim yourself to be or what you associate yourself with when God calls your name and presents his will to you, there is no backing down. Submission to the will opens doors to blessing and a life that is full of joy and peace. From my personal experience, when it comes to surrendering to the will of God and giving him a total "yes," I do not regret my decision, not one moment. For when I reflect and think about the honor bestowed upon me by God, who chose me to do his will, I am astounded. Yes, I have days that are longer than others, days where I may feel disappointed, and days where I am overjoyed, but I refuse to let anything dissuade me or take away my zeal for ministry and giving God a yes. Can you imagine what your life would be like if you give God a "no" and decide to continue down an ever-spiraling path that possibly leads to destruction, demise, confusion, unhappiness, and never-ending cycles of disappointment? Have you considered by now just how important and treasured your response to the call and will of God is, not just in but on your life? Maybe you need to take the time to consider the power of your "yes" and how it will make the difference in your life, your daily walk, and your relationship with Christ. The world maybe tempting you with the lusts of the flesh and eyes, but is it truly worth losing over your soul and position with Christ to satisfy mortal desires?

The Acceptance of God's Will

Beloved, let me tell you the truth. Our journey down here on earth only lasts as long as God ordains it, and we have been set upon this earth to heed his voice and beckoned call upon our lives. I want you to remember he has created each and every one of us for a special purpose, but he gives us the choice to decide if we want to:

- Follow him
- Obey his word
- Seek him daily
- Serve him wholeheartedly
- Do his will

God wants volunteers, not hostages. The choice is yours. Only you know the answer because he allows you the option to leave his flock and follow the ways of Satan and of the world. But you should be warned that if you decide to leave his flock, he is a shepherd who will come looking for his lost sheep. So never think you've gotten so far away from the grace of God that you cannot be redeemed or be welcomed back into the safety of his loving arms. I myself can testify how the ways of the world will trick you and set you up for destruction, making it look like following God and serving him are not worth your time or energy. But they show you glimpses of what you desire and mirages to tempt you, and pry you away from the grace of God and his will. Do not be fooled, my friend, or be persuaded to turn away from God for a disillusion that will only cause you heartache, pain, and trouble in the end. For me, I found myself tricked and fooled by the world so much, to take me away from what God had called me to do. It was to the point I became immature and found myself more concerned with the things of the world. I fell from the grace of God and found myself on my knees, begging for mercy as I prayed for help and understanding in what I was going through. And it was the comforter who stayed with me and helped to nurse me back to my right state of mind. I was sinking deep in sin and literally let the world overtake my mind to the point where I was no longer who I had claimed myself to be. But thanks be to a God, who sits so high but looks so low, that he found the time to redeem and rescue me from a whirlwind storm that had me trapped. My only goal in writing this book is to help someone else who may be feeling like they cannot fulfill the call and purpose God has destined for their lives, or are uncertain on which way they should turn. I want you to know today that God is on your side, working everything out for your good, and this, too, shall pass. I am a living testimony, and I can declare to everybody (this means you, too, devil) that I'm an overcomer! So do not give up, regardless of who you are or who you are called to be, but stand strong in the liberty, knowing God can use anybody in spite of who you are, if you are willing to give him your "yes."

CHAPTER 6

THERE'S PURPOSE IN THE PROCESS

There is a fast-food restaurant many of us have frequented quite often, known for a familiar slogan expressing to its customers that "you can have it your way." And although it is a nice thought, when you really think about life and how things proceed no one can have things "their way." Of course we, as human beings, like to think we can have things our way, or for that matter anything we want without cost, repercussions, or even great sacrifice.

But for those who believe such a crazy idea, I'd like to think that you are suffering from a delusional disorder wherein you have allowed unshakeable beliefs in something so untrue or not based upon reality, such as the idea that you can have anything your way. How foolishly have we allowed the world and Satan to convince us we have an automatic right to possession of whatever delights or satisfies us without realizing there is a process for everything in life. The world has become so adamant about satisfying itself that it has forgotten the power of the process.

Even so, do you not realize there is even a process to having things the way you want at this unnamed fast-food restaurant? The process begins with the order being taken, then the cashier repeats the order back to the customer, checking for errors, and payment follows next. Afterward someone then continues the process by preparing the food for the customer as they have requested. Once the food is prepared the process continues by packaging the finalized food items, retrieving beverages as requested, filling bags with paper goods and condiments before it is given to the customer. As you can see, this process has many steps and stages, which obviously do not signify anything about having something your way, demonstrating that no matter what we desire or want there is a process that we must undergo to attain anything we truly long or yearn for greatly.

And the same stands true for our walk with Christ. As we grow closer to God and come into the knowledge of who we are and who he has called us to be, he takes us through a process of purging, development, and establishment to prepare us for the work he has destined each one of us to perform. Process, an established, ever-evolving series of steps, is like a washing cycle. It goes through many stages before clothes are completely clean. Liken unto us we, too, go through many stages to help complete the process of God in us. There is no absolute time restraint when we are being taken through the process, as God has the final say and determination when we come forth complete and await his direction.

My high school years were the most adventurous but trying times for me, as I tried to find my identity and at the same time prove to the naysayers that I would be a success story as well as surpass the words of those who had spoken behavioral problems and an IEP, where they said one thing it wasn't until I came to the realization it was not what they said but what God said and I believed. When I denounced it, it fled. See, you need to understand and realize that ole' satan will try to throw you off course with a familiar attack but at a different time in your life to throw you off track. I should know because he tried to the same game with me in an attempt to distract and displace me from my purpose. He wants to make you believe you are predestined for failure and tries to infiltrate you to believe that you would be nothing more. There were days when I could hear my grandmother praying for me and calling out to the Lord for a change to take place. But what we must remember is that there is a process or order for everything. And even though some may have counted me out, such as teachers and friends, a change was soon to come. I started concentrating better and was able to complete assignments without struggle. I decided I was going to take control of my behavior and put my best effort forward every year of high school. What we forget is that when transition takes place we need to immediately establish a process or routine that will keep us focused and making progress.

Four years later, by the prayers of my grandmother, my hard work, and effort, I marched across the stage, graduating from high school with honors. Can you believe it? And to this day my grandmother still has the yellow honor chord from my graduation regalia as a memento of how the process prevailed. She's kept that chord to boast to others, and as a reminder that God has the final say. I am the first one to graduate from the collegiate level on my paternal side of the family. It's all in the process if you have faith and believe that there is a purpose for your process. I've even received my doctoral in divinity from the Redeemed Bible Seminary & Institute of Baltimore, Maryland. I still give God praise as I recall my recent 2017 graduation from Ashford University with a bachelor of arts in psychology. Therefore do not forsake the purpose; allow God to take you through the process to obtain your purpose. Your course of development may take longer than someone else's, but it is important during the process to be patient and realize God is at work, for as the scripture proclaims, "But let patience have her perfect work, that ye may be perfect and entire, wanting nothing" (James 1:4).

But the problem I have witnessed in ministry is when we finally cease from running, decide to follow Christ, and heed to his call we become so impatient with the next step we decide to skip the process and move straight for the glory. I find it interesting how there are so many preachers of the gospels who have created these self-proclaimed testimonials and stories of how they pulled themselves up from their own bootstraps and how they were struggling to survive. They "claim" they were so lost until Jesus called them and how he found them. And immediately after he called them, they started preaching and teaching the gospel with all this great conviction. Yet the issue is that everyone wants the glory, but no one wants to tell their story. Everyone desires the greatness but dismisses the process without realizing there is a purpose in the process. Remember there is purpose for everything even when it comes to process. A process is composed of organized steps that detail on every level what is expected and directives for successfully completing them. It is impossible to complete a process in one day, seeing that it is a gradual or staged series that continues to grow until completed. And we must master each stage of the process before we can be promoted to the next step.

A prime example of a process one cannot move too fast in completing is when it comes to fixing a recipe, especially one that involves baking. I myself dabble in baking and know that the process is one that takes time, skill, and patience for an end result to come out just right. You need all the ingredients (no substitutions), everything must be measured correctly, the oven temperature set just right, and the proper baking tools and utensils. This is just the first part of the process, getting what is properly needed to create a perfect final result. And with God's help he does the same thing by preparing us for the process to change, and it can be tedious, stressful, and, yes, even confusing, but you will prevail. Once the ingredients are gathered, the oven is preheating, and you have the utensils, it is time to start putting things together. Let us remember that when it comes to baking you cannot traditionally throw everything together and stick it in the pan. One must slowly combine the ingredients. And like the process with God you cannot move so quickly that you immediately rush to get the process completed. You must move in order and follow God's directions. Once the ingredients are combined and mixed exceptionally well, it is time to bake. But do not forget to grease the pan before you pour the batter in, or else it will stick.

Isn't it funny that even in cooking, oil is an essential ingredient? But in the spiritual sense God continues to move you through the process by drenching you in the oil, his anointing, which prepares you for the purpose he has set for you. I want you to know that in spite of this process you are covered and anointed to do the work of the Almighty God, therefore fear not. Once the pan is greased and the batter poured, then it can be placed in the oven for the set time to bake. As part of us undergoing the process of transformation and establishment, God shapes us by placing us in his heavenly mold, and then like the potter with the clay he puts us in the fire so that we can be purged, formed, and solidified in our purpose to complete his will. Yes, it will be hot, but I promise you the fire is for your betterment and not intended to harm you but help you. Finally, after a set time, the final product, which can be smelled throughout the area, is taken out to cool. Can you smell God doing something new with you, too? Once the cake is cooled one can then put icing on it and then present it to others to enjoy. The final stage of his process is literally the icing on top of the cake as he puts extras in and on you, which are your spiritual gifts specifically prepared and picked for your ministry and purpose, set by God before he presents you to the world. You see, beloved, without process there can be no purpose, therefore allow God to take you through the process so that you may be able to fulfill your purpose. It is never an overnight journey, but in the end you will be better than you started.

Would you believe I had such a hard time coming into the will of Christ and accepting his process for my life? I tried to fight the process any way I could and ended up making it longer and more painful for me. I know God was trying to discipline me and show me direction for my life so that I'd be prepared for ministry better, but I thought I knew what was best for me, and was I ever so wrong. Never doubt God in the process because you will not make it to your purpose on time and gain your promise. I myself get all too eager when it comes to the word "process," and God has reminded me continuously as he has said in Jeremiah 29:11: "For I know the thoughts that I think toward you, saith the Lord, thoughts of peace, and not of evil, to give you an expected end."

When I think about this scripture it helps me to understand more about process and how God has already ordained plans for us that will help us prosper and succeed without bringing harm to us. Remember when walking through the process, God sets the pace for your life, not you. It is imperative that you follow the process as he guides you through it. Don't be doing just to do; do it with a purpose. Because where he has set you at this juncture of your life is no coincidence.

Principle #6
Where You Are Is Not a Coincidence!

As humans, process is series of events that we undergo, but there comes a time to realize that aside from the process, where you are is not a coincidence. God will place you during the "process" stage of your life in a position where your placement is not just by chance but for a specific season. We've seen throughout the Bible where God's divine and infinite will had placed people in maybe odd or irregular positions, but we learn that where they were was not just by chance. See, in God's will, his way, and his mind, position is key in the plan he has for all of us. A prime example is the position of the "woman with the issue of blood." Don't you find it ironic that she happened to be by "chance" in the right place at the right time for the right blessing? Look through your own life and incidents that have taken place at various times. Was it a coincidence you happened to be placed or positioned there?

- Assisting a frantic coworker who dislikes you but in need of prayer
- Moving into a neighborhood where you are the only minority
- Placed on a job where many are participants in an opposing religion

There's Purpose in the Process

Sometimes we ask God, "Why am I here and not there?" but realize it's by chance or coincidence he's put you in a specific place for a specific reason, for a specific blessing, lesson, or ministerial opportunity. We never know just why God positions us, but when he does there is a reason and, yes, a season to be in that place. And part of the purpose for your process in learning to accept the will of God is understanding there is a purpose in your placement and that you're not there by mistake.

When I started preaching the gospel of Christ and received my first official assignment, I was outraged instead of ecstatic. I felt where they had positioned me was beneath me and my calling in ministry. I tried to get out of it but no one wanted to switch with me, and my senior elder plainly said to me, "Son, where you've been positioned is never a choice but rather a divine assignment to develop, grow, and prepare you for the greater work God has called and destined you for." In my human mind I still refused to believe the words, but out of obedience I humbly obliged. As I reflect how I won more souls for Christ in completing this assignment, not because of who I was but because I had been placed there for a reason, and come to find out it was my openness, honesty, exuberance, and charisma that positioned me to open the hearts of the hurting and forgotten that won them over to Christ's side. Thinking back, I was positioned not by man but by God, because he knew this opportunity was one only someone in my shoes, who had been forsaken, misunderstood, suffered great loss, and so on, could complete. I learned from that day to never reject the coincidence of the position, but instead to let it guide me to my purpose while undergoing the process.

In the eighth chapter of the gospel of Mark, right around the twenty-second verse, we see a prime example of the principle "where you are is not a coincidence" as we meet a blind man who had been blind since birth. This blind man was apparently hanging out with friends who just so happened to have decided to take an alternate route to get to the town of Bethsaida. He knew his way around regardless of sight; his other senses were heightened. He probably protested the alternate route, stating they were taking the "long way" around. However, it appeared that by chance where he ended up was not where he planned to be, but it looked as if he had a predestined meeting with Christ. Saints, God will meet you whether you refuse to meet him. He will find you when you cannot find him, to guide you as you proceed through the process of becoming who he has destined you to become. The chance meeting in this case between the blind man and Jesus was not just a coincidence but an encounter that would direct him from a place of darkness and into a path of light and enlightenment.

When we decide to refuse to undergo the process of becoming who we are destined to become, we deny the purpose in our lives for living. What I want everyone to understand is that as you undergo the process, no matter how tedious, frustrating, confusing, or even lengthy, there is a purpose in it. The purpose being that like this blind man God is delivering you from your old ways of thinking, living, reacting, and being, a path of darkness, and through his purposeful process, pushing you into the light.

Now this "blind man" had no sight, and the Bible gives no reason or alludes to specifics on how or when he became blind, but we are assuming he was born this way. Side note: just because you make the claim, "I was born this way," it does not necessarily separate you from the call of duty to serve Christ, or even submit humbly to his will. I should let you know that as you undergo the process of rebirth and renewal to become who God has truly designed you to be, in time you will realize how you were born has no effect on the calling upon your life. And by him being blind this man had no sight, but as for you, beloved, your blindness may not be pertaining to sight, but you could be suffering from blindness in other ways or senses.

- Spiritual blindness (you have lost sight of who God is exactly and the role he plays in your life, and thus you are unable to establish a functioning a relationship with Christ)
- Mental blindness (things are blocking and blinding your ability to focus clearly to produce sensible thoughts and actions)

Back to the story this "blind man" and his friends, they ended up in Bethsaida and heard the whispers of a man who could heal the lame and the sick, and reverse death. They decided themselves that they had to help their friend. Hmm, isn't it interesting how they put their friends needs above their own wants? Question, are you around those who are willing to help you through the process to push you to your next level? Or are you surrounded by those who will push you from your process and keep you down? When you are going through a process, you do not need everyone surrounding you and interfering with you while you attempt to get your deliverance. Be cautious of who's surrounding you, because everyone who claims to help you may not really be there to help but hinder you from your place of development. This blind man allowed his friends to lead him, and ironically, after hearing the testimonials they led him straight to the King of kings, Jesus.

Side note: real friends lead you to help that will be an everlasting savior and life saver! (wink).

Jesus willingly obliged to heal this "blind man," but he did it outside of his environment by removing him from anything that could hinder him and make him change his mind or even look back. For some of us, having the option or even the opportunity to ponder, glance, or just have a quick reminiscent moment in our past brings reservations, hindrances, and road blocks that alter our way of thinking, moving, and doing, to the point where it tempts us to want to go back instead of moving forward. The word clearly states, "…come out from among them, and be ye separate..." (2 Corinthians 6:17). God led him past everything he knew, into a newness that would set him free and open his eyes. God is doing the same to you as he walks you and leads you through your process, into the destiny customized just for you. Secondly you, like the blind man, cannot get your healing while hanging in the past environment that traps you in blindness instead of opening your eyes and gifting you with the blessedness of sight. For example, one cannot get clean while bathing with the same dirty rag.

- Gossip
- Sin
- Jealousy
- Strife
- Anger
- Cursing
- Lust
- Fornication
- Stealing
- Cheating

The word lets us know in Revelation 21:5 that, "...I make all things new," and the word new means being made fresh, thus coming into recent existence. He takes us like this blind man and sets us free from the bondage of our past, making us fresh and entering into a renewed, unpolluted existence/being of our former selves while undergoing the process. You see, coming out is a process that, as the scripture mentions, does not take overnight. Everyone does not undergo the same process to becoming new, because process is something that is ever evolving. And as you undergo it you yourself are ever changing and evolving into a better, newer you who God can use and identify as his own. What you need to remember is that while you are in the process you do not have a hold of God, because your grip just may slip, but he has a hold of you. The word tells us in Mark 8:23 that Jesus, for a prime example, took a hold of him (the "blind" man), thus allowing God to touch this man. Note: he touched him more than once to get his healing, and the first touch God uses in the text was not so much about healing as it was Jesus' effort to build and establish a relationship with this man.

It is through the establishment of a:

- True
- Real
- Faithful
- Daily
- Dedicated

relationship that one can be changed as they undergo the process because they are:

- Reading his word
- Praying constantly
- Seeking his will
- Conversing with him daily
- Serving wholeheartedly

which will lead to purpose in the process, and it is something so valuable one cannot afford to lose.

For the first time he saw, although he couldn't see clearly, but it was through the establishment of that relationship that he was gifted with a chance to see again. It took a second time. Hmm, doesn't God give us second chances? Christ did it again, and this time had him look up. But didn't David proclaim, "I will lift up mine eyes to the hills from which cometh my help"? And this was when he gained his sight, looking up to the hills, and he received his help.

Lift up your head and be lifted up…for the King of Glory came into his life purposefully establishing a new relationship through the process that granted this man sight. Had he not looked up, would he have gained his sight? Again one cannot say, but he stopped looking down from that day hence and kept looking up regardless of:

- Fear
- Doubt
- Stress
- Worry
- Hardships
- Intimidations
- Disappointments

And it granted him the ability, with Jesus' touch, to see like he'd never seen or beheld things before. Theologians will tell you God works in threes, because the number three represents unity. And throughout the retelling of this biblical text, God demonstrates his omniscient power to work in threes by:

1. Taking the blindness out of his environment
2. Spitting on his eyes the first time to heal him
3. Putting his hands upon his eyes a second time to clarify the "blind" man's sight

There's Purpose in the Process

And liken unto theologians, one can testify that by God working in threes, according to the scripture:

1. He took three disciples
2. He had three bear witness on earth
3. Man himself is made up of three—mind, body, and spirit

I want you to see for yourself and realize that God is a keeper who will sustain you where you are until he can get you into that place of restoration and revelation. And once you are positioned, he then can begin to expose to you what he has in store for you. In the end once this former "blind man" was healed, he was directed to not return into the town of Bethsaida and not tell anyone in that town what transpired between him and Christ. You see, his process did not require one to boast or loudly proclaim change, but instead, as the scripture states in Matthew 5:16: "Let your light so shine before men, that they may see your good works, and glorify your Father which is in heaven." And this man complied obediently as he took an alternate route home, and probably, while some may have marveled in his hometown about his miraculous healing, he kept the details and gossip on how his redemption came about. But I guarantee you he was able to be a living witness and demonstration of the miracle and power of the purpose in the process God has designed and carefully orchestrated for each one of you. So it's not so much what you're going through as much as where you are presently and where he has provisionally destined for you to go. There never are coincidences with Christ, but simple incidental encounters that are life-changing.

Am I Ready Now?

As I reflect today, I realize how God is a true keeper in everything.

- Through the storms of life
- Through the trials that come
- Through the unexpected situations that arise
- Through the pain and frustration adversity brings

I don't know about you, but no matter what in the mist of everything he is truly an awesome and amazing God. I don't know about you, but is there anybody who can say God has taken care of me while I was blinded? What one should realize is that when you are blind you are not able to see and everything is dark, blurry, and unrecognizable. You may still be blinded if:

- You are still in the club
- You are still fornicating
- You are still drinking
- You are still disobedient
- You are still backbiting

But there is a way of escape, and he is waiting for you to take his hand and allow him to lead you from your past and into your future. Be glad and rejoice because even in your blindness, did you forget that He was still talking care of you and leading you? Be honest, no one else was there and it takes true dedication to care for someone who's so wounded that they've become blinded beyond repair. I want you to know that like in the scriptural text, every touch has a test. Note: in the gospel of Mark chapter 8, verse 23, when he touched him, he asked the blind man, "What did he see?" I want you to know when you enter that state of newness and receive your healing, you will be tested. Therefore upon taking his hand and giving him your heart, kindly oblige his assistance and remain resilient by repeating his word, meditate upon it day and night, pray constantly, but let not fear give place to the devil. It's your time now to walk into a season of newness and servanthood. Know not of your past, but that he's given you an expected end that will catapult you into greatness beyond that which you will ever know. See, sometimes God will push you from one place to another. He will push you from the old, your past, and the familiar environment and into a place of brightness, new sight, new focus, and new attitude to do his will without fear, resolve, and or uncertainty.

Do not give into your feelings so that what you have received will not, in this case, become dim, unusable, and you are once again left in the dark, searching to find your way. I myself have experienced that blindness and found myself wandering in a darkness that seemed to go on for eternity, but once I took his hand my eyes were opened to a newness like never before. I may have been hesitant, but to be delivered from the darkness and brought into the marvelous light is an experience one never forgets because redemption doesn't often come, yet chaos and confusion can last a lifetime. So I ask you today, are you ready to take his hand to leave the old but familiar? Or are you careless enough to remove your hand from his grip, trapping you in an eternal disillusioned reality of what your life could be? I can only provide you the facts to help guide you in your decision-making process; this choice is solely up to you. I made mine some time ago, but today, right now, the choice is up to you. What's yours?

CHAPTER 7

THE REVEALING

Throughout this book I've given you principles that will help you gain insight on who you are in Christ and who God wants you to be, but now it is time for you to take the final step into your destiny to become who and what he's called you to be… "a new creature in Christ" (2 Corinthians 5:17). But now is the time for the revealing to take place and so, as they say in sports, "The ball is in your court!" Are you ready to forsake the world and take the hand of Christ, leading you into a new dimension of spirituality and revelation as he unveils in you and through you the divinely formed individual and vessel he has carefully crafted just as the potter crafts the clay he has called to do his will? Then this is your revealing. It's time.

This is God's opportunity to make known to all the world through divine inspiration what he has chosen, such a one as you to be. Do you remember Moses? He was born like you, with a destiny to be fulfilled by God's divine planning and will. And you, too, like Moses, may have been or may be:

- Abandoned
- Given up on
- Raised differently
- Confused about your identity
- Running from your past, present, or future
- Looking for fulfillment in other ventures
- Unsure of your destiny
- Trying to fit in a place you don't belong
- Unfamiliar with your next place in life

But after today it shall be revealed that through his glory and divine plan, he has called you to serve him.

When I think about my beginning and where I started and now look at where I am now, I marvel at the wonderful change God has worked in me, through me, and for me. I grew up with a life of adversity and challenge, but through Christ I was able to conqueror them all. But one of the most difficult challenges was dealing with the pain of losing my mother when I was only six years old. It was a period of life I felt down and like I was not wanted. Even at that age I questioned God why he would take my mother from me and my younger sister. Having to deal with my own mother's death made me feel lost, forsaken, and yes, even forgotten by God. But then the times really got tough because three years later, when I was nine years old, he took my father as well. I spent many nights questioning my grandmother, sobbing on her lap, not understanding the purpose he had for me and all this tragedy. My grandmother, being a praying woman, simply stated, "It shall be revealed."

I never understood and would be frustrated, but today I understand and clearly see the bigger picture. I see how God was preparing me for calling, my destiny, and ordering my steps all at the same time. It was then I came to know him as a keeper, healer, and friend. And I can attest today He led me right into the purpose for my life. You see, sometimes God does not reveal his will or plans to and us immediately, but in time he shows us what exactly he has for us. See, God is the master potter and he was building me a resistance to be stronger so that when adversity and challenges came I could take on the burden without breaking down. He wanted me to be prepared for any and everything that may hinder my journey to fulfilling his purpose and destiny he declared for my life. What I lost as a child helped push me to greatness, and I thank him for that because now I understand not just what it means when things shall be revealed, but what exactly is the revealing. The final revelation of all the making, prodding, preparation, and work coming forth into a divinely shaped and crafted vessel for the glory of God. For I shall be revealed. What about you?

Saints, you've been on that potter's wheel for way too long, avoiding the process of becoming who he has called you to be. Now is the time to cease from your running and allow God to undertake you for fine crafting. "But now, O LORD, thou art our father; we are the clay, and thou our potter; and we all are the work of thy hand" (Isaiah 64:8). No longer should you be continually spinning around and around as a moist, damp, sticky lump of earthen clay without form or figure. But God has stepped in and taken the time as a potter does, by sitting at that potter's wheel to take the time with you and mold you into who he has ordained you to be. He has spent the last few years, months, and days taking his time to shape you, mold you, form and develop you into his personal sacred vessel. For the word clearly states in Jeremiah 18:6: "Behold, as the clay is in the potter's hand, so are ye in mine hand..." Yes, he may have had some instances where when he started to create like any potter, you had to be made over more than it could be counted, but it was his holy design and strategy to perfect you according to his desire. And today I declare, my sister, my brother, you are finished.

I know there may have been days clouded with precipitation, but the potter needed to moisten the clay, so he could form you and position you just right for his divine destiny. By him pouring the living waters upon you, he is able to transform and rejuvenate you in preparation for the process of shaping, molding, and making you into a perfectly crafted vessel. He has taken the time to form you according to his passion and his will, so that there will be no imperfections or mistakes. God has removed all the impurities and possible pockets of air that have led to doubt, obstruction, and distraction, so that when he formed you, you are no longer susceptible to this world but that of his world. He's crafted you from the finest earthen clay, remaking, shaping, trimming, and adding all possible chances of resistance, fear, doubt, and uncertainty that could possibly hinder your servanthood and willingness to humbly accept his call. Liken unto the potter, he has repeatedly taken his time, willing to restart over and over as he gives you chance after chance after chance so that you are prepared and he no longer has to wait for you, because after that final touch he now says, "You are ready."

He's poured and covered you in the blood of Christ for redemption's sake, his sweat that is the tool to making you over, and his precious tears that dissolve all worries in you. He is ready to complete you, his masterpiece, by allowing you to dry before you can be fired. And, yes, there may have been times when it seemed like during this process things may have gotten more difficult, or you may have felt a little lonelier. But, baby, it's just the drying process! You see, in the art of ceramics once a vessel has been formed and crafted it cannot be immediately fired, and neither can you. The potter places the piece on the shelf to undergo the process of drying, and for some of you that may be where you find yourself right now. Do not worry. There is always a purpose in the process! You see, it's simply a period when all remaining moisture is removed; if not, when the piece comes out of the fire it could possibly crumble and not be able to withstand the world or take on its complete structure without falling apart.

So he puts you in a deserted place to help you release all that may cause you to turn and run. It is an opportunity to stand firm and a period of testing, when those who do not understand may bring:

- Frustration
- Confusion
- Disillusion
- Allegations
- Craziness

And they target you, but it's through this process that God is able to make you strong as you pour out all of what's been holding you from taking on the form and figure of who he has called you to be. How can you be ready when you're not even prepared to sit and let every possible hindrance be delivered from you? Yes, rain falls in your life but there are seasons of drying out or drought, where he allows you to sit and wait on him for direction, as everything in your environment and lifestyle are being removed from your life.

For me this was the hardest possible process he took me through, but I now understand his divine reasoning and exactly how it made me the man I am today. I learned we get so filled up with worldly distractions, cares, and ideologies that we allow them to displace us and weigh us down with perspirations of frustration, stress, anger, and ignorance; the list goes on and on to the point where we find ourselves unable to take on the shape or form of the character he has longed for you and I to become. But ha, ha, ha, ha! God is not finished with you yet, for as the potter he cannot expose a masterpiece until it has gone through the process after the drying-out period—the firing.

I know it has been or will be a very trying time, but in order to be revealed God must put you through the fire. The firing. It is the process of purification, perfecting, and purging. It's not an easy process to undergo and, yes, it's going to get hot, but stay strong and know it's all for your good and betterment. Let the master potter complete his work on and in you, for it is in the firing process, as the time of revealing nears, he places you in the spiritual kiln to remove you from:

- The cares of this world that have held you down
- Friends and family who obscure your vision
- Environmental distractions that push you from your purpose
- Spiritual hindrances that stunt your growth and development
- Anything that possibly leads you from the calling and into a disillusioned mind-set

But one thing you must remember is to stand still until God's process is complete. Realize, my child, that you are undergoing the firing and purification process so that when he reveals you to the world, once the process has been completed, no one will be able to say anything about:

- What you were
- Who you were

- Who you were with
- What you "used" to do or be
- How you used to be

Remember he has the power to hide the evidence from everyone and "No weapon that is formed against thee shall prosper; and every tongue *that* shall rise against thee in judgment thou shalt condemn" (Isaiah 54:17). He is a God who knows all and he understands how the enemy works through the human mind to spread guilt, fear, remorse, worry, and trepidation, but thanks be to him who cause us to triumph over any and all adversities. He has the power to make all things new and that means you, too! Why worry when God is on your side and he has chosen you for such a time as this? It's simply the process of refreshing in your life:

- Spiritual refreshing
- Mental refreshing
- Physical refreshing

It is not a short process, but when you come forth you will be revealed as a new babe in Christ, ready to do his will. The final process is one that is composed of two parts, where during part one God puts you through the firing process of purification and purging. Then comes the second part of his process and plan known as the cooling-off period. It is a process where he personally allows you to sit and take in everything that is to come. He gives one the opportunity to reflect on all you have been through and everything you're being prepared to endure, as well as his goodness, mercy, loving-kindness, and grace. This cool-off period or process is vital because you are given the chance for reflection as you prepare for you assignment selection. It is not a very long time one must undergo, but it is adequate to permit you an opportunity to present yourself to your Savior as a living sacrifice, holy and acceptable, willing to serve and take on the special task God has called you to do.

For in a matter of time the master potter is coming to present and introduce you for all to see; it is your time of revealing, your second opportunity to come forth from amongst the rubble, dust, and those who didn't make it. As with all potters they are most critical of their own creations, and God must sometimes make drastic decisions when it comes to who and whom he can use for his master plan. Of course there may have been others selected, but as the potter placed them on the wheel they could not be molded, shaped, or guided, so he disposed of them. Or ones who may have started out with you during the process but did not make the cut. And then there are a few like you who were called, had the opportunity to give God a yes, made it through the entire process, only to get to the end and refuse. But on the other hand, it may have been a case where he had some "perpetrators," "fake," or even "phony" who may have claimed to have the holy ghost, the fruits of the spirit, faith, love…but these did not make it, either. He saw how they cracked under pressure in the spiritual kiln or while undergoing the process of drying because of all the insincerity and "fakeness" they role-played in declaring who they were.

All those fakers who did more talking, you know, the ones working who are complainers, the ones who acted like they're doing something, the ones who always volunteer to be seen, when the time of revealing comes, God, being the great revelator and divine being he is, shows everything. But these people, instead of being found out, crack under the pressure to either cease, obey, and serve or to enter into the path of unrighteousness. In the end all is revealed and he realizes who and whom he can use. And one thing one must understand is that God calls but he never begs. Aren't you glad the potter didn't dispose of you during the process? My advice to you "…my beloved brethren, be ye stedfast, unmoveable, always abounding in the work of the Lord, forasmuch as ye know that your labour is not in vain in the Lord" (1 Corinthians 15:58). There are others he could call to take your place as you stand foolishly looking around, losing everything he's blessed you with, and that means possibly your life.

For someone as myself I had to realize that this is a process of development that only the strong and faithful can survive. I was fearful and made more excuses than I'd like to let the world know, but God took me through this journey and stayed with me every step of the way. Like the hymnologist states, "And he walks with me and he talks with me…," together with God by my side I made it and I survived! And I began to develop a stronger relationship with God, finding myself growing closer to him every day. The scripture says to "seek him daily," and I began to form a more solidified and intimate relationship by going to him and he no longer had to look for me.

As I underwent this intense remaking he not only changed my walk, my talk, but he changed my thoughts, too. I started seeking his glory and my mind-set was no longer worried about the world, but more on the word and how I could do the will of the one who sent me. I desired to please him and no longer gave in to my selfish desires to please myself, because I was undergoing the process of reformation by the master potter himself. I still cannot believe how the potter took someone like me, a wretch undone, and formed me into a beautiful, divinely created masterpiece for his will and way. And, yes, like some of you I started out with fellow peers who "claimed" to be faithful to the holy cause and gave their all for Christ, but as time progressed and the requests from God got more demanding in the formation process, they chickened out and ran. But me, here I am, and thanks be to God who causes me to triumph!

Regardless of what I had to go through, I'll let you know that your process may not be like mine but it is all a part of his divine plan. And when God reveals you he makes everything that has been hidden, secret, or secluded known to all. You shall come forth as pure gold, renewed, refreshed, and rejuvenated, prepared for your calling. And I want to tell you running never profits you anything. So be strong in the Lord and the power of his might, knowing that as this monumental process concludes you will be a new creature in Christ, ready for the task he has specifically ordained for someone like you. Others have left or fallen by the wayside of their foolish actions and reprobate minds, but here you stand today, able to say, "Lord, here I am, ready to do your will. I accept the task you have for me. Yes, your ways are not my ways, but I am ready to concede my will to yours." The revealing is a process for some that may take more time, and for others less, but I have learned that he customizes the process to his needs, desires, and wants that he has for each and every one of us. So fear not and stand still to see the salvation of the Lord with your hands lifted and your mind set to believing. "I can do all things through Christ who strengthens me." For you shall be revealed. Are you ready?

Principle #7
You Shall Come Forth!

Such a simple and yet powerful phrase, the final principle I've been asked to give his children. As I complete this chapter I want you to know that "forth" means to move onward in time, place, and order. Simply put, it's a season to move forward. Putting your past as well as your old self away because it is time to put on the new man. You are coming forth to proclaim the mighty hand and power of God to the uttermost. So in this final chapter, as you prepare to fulfill the total destiny of kingdom servanthood, I want you to look at one specific instance from the Bible to help you fully understand the power to come forth.

One of the first things you need to understand is that where you are is no coincidence. I say this because look where you are right this very moment. Is it possible you were supposed to be:

- In jail
- In a mental institute
- Six feet under, in your grave
- In a drug house, out of your mind
- Still in that abusive relationship
- Homeless
- Penniless
- Broke, busted, and disgusted
- Unemployed

But is it possible God gave you the miracle of the Passover? That's right. God, like the children of Israel who were in Egypt, allowed you to escape it all in a Passover. My God, my God. You look back and wonder how you made it when others who were around you at that time or this time long ago are either dead, trapped in an unproductive lifestyle, are unhappy, and stagnated. But you, my God, he let all of that pass over you! He covered you with the blood of the lamb so that no death, danger, or harm would come to you and your dwelling place. He sounded the alarm to prevent any touching of you from spiritual, demonic attacks, for the scripture clearly states, "Touch not mine anointed, and do my prophets no harm" (1 Chronicles 16:22). Hallelujah! The gift of Passover has brought you out and led you out of the land of Egypt (corruption, evil, enslavement) to a place of freedom, rejuvenation, liberty, and opportunity. Take your newfound opportunity that he's given you to realize there is a reason why he spared someone such as yourself. And now you are coming through and forth new, a creature in Christ. He let you be passed over to bring you into the will and way he's personally prepared for you in anticipation of your devotion and service to him. Others didn't make it, but I'm so glad you did. Aren't you glad to be in his service?

My sisters and my brothers, as I think back and revisit the inner memories of my mind, I give God glory for his never-ceasing saving power and how he offered me that rare chance of a Passover deliverance from the temptations of this world and into his army and service. I thought I would lose so much in telling him yes, but in reality I have gained more than I ever could from the blessings, his favor, mercy, love everlasting, loving-kindness, peace of mind, comfort, and friendship. If I hadn't taken the Passover when offered to me, I doubt there would have been a second chance because Passover only occurred one time. That holy and sanctified celebration may be commemorated yearly, but it has yet to this day have reoccurred. So when God offers you the opportunity, not of a "do-over" but a "Passover," let him cover you in his sacred blood and deliver you out of the hands of the enemy and into his loving, compassionate arms of freedom. Celebrate your Passover!

I want you to know right now that you shall come forth, and what

God has destined for your life shall come forth. What God has for you will prevail. Beloved, you shall come forth over adversities, trials, and tribulations. You see, just like the children of Israel came forth without hurt, harm, or danger, you shall come forth, too. I know it seems like he has assigned you a task that may appear to be impossible for you, but know that God looks at the heart and sees your passion to succeed and please him. He only picks the fruit he can use that is viable, fresh, energizing, and ripe. If you can endure it, you can come forth through it and he will help you.

Now is the time to position yourself. How can you come forth if you are not in the right position? Even the children of Israel had to be in position during the Passover to receive the blessing. When it came time for David to be anointed king, he was where God ordained him to be, not in the front but in the field working. God is looking for those who are willing to forsake being seen but would rather be found working for his kingdom. Be like David and know who you are and whose you are regardless of where you have been placed to work. Let God find you. Openly ask him, "Lord, what is your will for me?" and I guarantee he will direct you and lead you. There are some he called to be preachers, some he called to be evangelists, some he called to be deacons, and others he called to be missionaries, but regardless of where he has called you to work know he has something for you to do. So I urge you to get into position, because you've endured the Passover and now is the time that you shall come forth.

CONCLUSION

THE DECISION

I want you to remember that this decision is yours. You've been presented with a divine opportunity—it's up to you to accept. Just know that for every divine opportunity God always gives provisions. Therefore do not worry about what you may face or what may come your way; he's got your back. Honesty and holy boldness will open the door to divine blessings. It's okay to be yourself because God is looking for you and no one else. Never be ashamed of who you are and what you've endured. God always hides the glory behind the story. So I ask, "Whom do you choose to serve this day?"

Know that this is your time and your day to yield and surrender to the will of the Great I Am, or remain stuck in a reprobate mind and lifestyle without prosperity, peace, and joy. This walk is one that you will have to take on your own. It will be a trying time, but I guarantee when you give God a yes, he makes all things possible. Now is the time to determine the season of your life that you desire to walk into boldly, without regret.

- Is this your season to persevere and walk into your calling, accepting only what God allows?
- Are you ready to give him a "yes"?
- Is today your day to give him your hand and your heart?

It's up to you to change the season of your life. If you can bring your mind to conceive it, allow yourself to believe it, and then you will receive it. I urge you to walk into your destiny knowing already you have decided within your heart to accept this season of the unfamiliar and newness, accepting his will, and obediently giving him a yes to the call he has placed upon your life. Beloved, even the prodigal son decided his season had ended and it was time to move on.

The scripture states, "My people are destroyed for lack of knowledge…" (Hosea 4:6). For everything God has created is good and he has an assignment for you. One that has been designed, crafted, and created for someone like you that no one else on this earth can fulfill. He has ordained this special task just for you. Today is your day to go boldly in his renewing mercies, knowing that he picked someone as cherished as you to fulfill his will.

Go boldly, go bravely, but above all go prayerfully, knowing you will be able to admit to yourself as well to Christ your Savior, "Now, I'm ready!"

CPSIA information can be obtained
at www.ICGtesting.com
Printed in the USA
LVHW082017311019
636002LV00002B/2/P